It's Not About The Coach

Getting the most from coaching in business, sport and life

T0096986

It's Not About The Coach

Getting the most from coaching in business, sport and life

Stuart Haden

BUSINESS BOOKS

Winchester, UK
Washington, USA

First published by Business Books, 2013
Business Books is an imprint of John Hunt Publishing Ltd., Laurel House, Station Approach,
Alresford, Hants, SO24 9JH, UK
office1@jhpbooks.net
www.johnhuntpublishing.com

For distributor details and how to order please visit the 'Ordering' section on our website.

Text copyright: Stuart Haden 2012

ISBN: 978 1 78099 642 4

All rights reserved. Except for brief quotations in critical articles or reviews, no part of this
book may be reproduced in any manner without prior written permission from the publishers.

The rights of Stuart Haden as author have been asserted in accordance with the Copyright,
Designs and Patents Act 1988.

A CIP catalogue record for this book is available from the British Library.

Design: Stuart Davies

Printed and bound by CPI Group (UK) Ltd, Croydon, CR0 4YY

We operate a distinctive and ethical publishing philosophy in all
areas of our business, from our global network of authors to
production and worldwide distribution.

CONTENTS

Coaching is a space between two or more people. This is a story about the coachee. Inspiring them to...
Make informed choices about coaching - possibilities
Discover readiness for learning - perception
Develop the values required for success - performance

Part 1 – What's it About?

Search for the hero

It's not about the coach. Already you have formed an opinion of what it's not about. This is intentional, you have begun to create your own meaning. Using your own thoughts, ideas and language. Not mine, yours. Herein lies the energy, within you, not me. A classic concept that is found in coaching, your agenda, not someone else's. You know it's not about the coach so you have sidelined a number of different areas, thus narrowing the playing field. At the start of this journey I encourage you to hold onto your views. As soon as I start to tell you what it is about then you will begin to identify one way or another with what I say. Which is fine also, but don't loose sight of your own path.

When transformation takes place, you need to be clear on what it's not about. Then you will know if you have strayed off the path. Equally you also need to find the hero of the story, what it is about. Thus you end up with what you don't want and what you do want.

My journey to find what I wanted began where many trips set out from these days, trying to second-guess a search engine. 'Did you mean reachability?' it inquires. Aren't I the one asking the question? Coachability, the ability to be coached. The capability to be coached, a talent that enables achievement. Are you 'coachable?' Words that are clumsy, words that are new. The landscape is being explored, not yet developed in our vocabulary. We are getting closer. It's about getting the most from coaching, from the learner's perspective.

Our hero is reading these pages, you. This story is about you. Who should read this? You. Why? Because we all end up in coaching situations from time to time. Thus we all need to get the best from these conversations that focus on improved performance. The hero inside yourself.The coachee, and their innate ability to develop coachability. Be coachable. A natural inborn value, our thirst for learning. Let's get coachees out in the open, the real heroes.

The hero's challenge

We find coachees in coaching relationships, it's recognised in our lives and work more now than it ever has been. It has always been practiced, now it is starting to receive greater recognition in business, sport and life. After all the role of a coach is in the running for being the oldest profession in the world. Yes, prostitution, acting and others also have nominations for this award. But, a one to one conversation with development as its focus is as old as the wheels we have reinvented. That's just it, we need some invention. The landscape is by definition ancient in its heritage, yet some unexplored areas remain, we have assumed so much. The coachee; a word that struggles to define its meaning. We have assumed that coachees will be OK, when they often are not.

You can make a start if you are anybody. Anybody who is involved in coaching. Primarily we focus our efforts on the coachee. You know this already. After all coaching meets the needs of the coachee, so the spotlight could be focused in their direction. Carefully, so we do not cast a shadow on the rest of the stage and our players. Remember, we are all coachees. You might also hold the role of coach, manager, leader, board member, back room staff or shareholder. Despite these responsibilities you will still need to appreciate the values associated with developing coachability. Pass a copy of this resource on to your coachee, so that they can develop choices associated with coaching, it will allow them to get ready for coaching it will develop their values.

Just because we have a hero does not mean we have a villain. Coachee and coach form the very special relationship. Add in two dimensions that describe this relationship and you are left with four areas of concern. Coachee - connection - coach - context. Call them what you want. A *coachee*, our learner. The *connection* between them both. Flow, chemistry, link, relation, association, bond, tie. In connection with the coachee you have the *coach*. Primarily responsible for holding the space for learning. Questions, listens, observes, feedback. In *context*, the circumstances that form the setting for the relationship. Together, woven, conditions, factors, situation, background, scene, setting, subject, theme, topic.

The connections and context are local, sometimes forming the process of coaching. Important, but not the be all and end all. The range of resources for coaches is vast. Bookshelves are bowing under their weight, e-readers allow one to consume multiple types of content. Coach qualifications, accreditation and supervision are all rising to meet this need. We go to great lengths to train, educate and develop individuals in the skills to become coaches, yet we do very little for the other half of the relationship. Even this percentage split is misleading. Physically the coachee makes up 50 per cent of the conversations but we should attribute more value than a half way split.

At the foundation lies the coachee, that's why they are first on our list. The connection, coach and context can all follow. Any effective relationship should have more of the focus with the coachee, the coach and process can sit very much in the background. So if we are missing out on perhaps over 50 per cent of the relationship, how come so many of these conversations can produce fantastic results? Well, as coachees gain coaching experience of course they also develop the values to be effective. But when? After their second conversation, half way through the season or ten years down the line? We are like-minded time travelers, so let's consider accelerated journeys that still vibrate with quality.

Accelerate the coachee's ability to develop their values. This is in essence is the ability to learn. Given that coaching is often one to one in nature it just happens to be one of the most pronounced learning experiences. Therefore, these values can be applied to any area in which we learn either by ourselves or with others. You will know when you get there when you begin to experience the ability to self-coach. This may happen whether you are working with a coach or simply undertaking individual learning. When you consider these words I hope you will get to the point of self-coaching quicker than if you were to embark on the journey alone. We are looking to increase the odds of coaching success by focusing in the right areas.

Those that can self-coach understand the choices available to them, they are ready for the coaching and they possess the necessary skills to make a fantastic coachee. These individuals have learnt these skills in a variety of ways and for a variety of reasons. The ability to hold onto possibilities, work with their perception and commit to action, which changes their performance. At the higher end of the scale they can deliver some of these changes without the need for a coach. Equally they can still self-coach in the presence of a coach. Often this develops towards the end of a coaching relationship.

Bring it to the table earlier than it would otherwise, self-coaching, developed earlier and further. This does not sideline the coach, remember there is no villain in our story. Two people are always more likely to harness more energy than one. Coaching is likely to lead to the development of precise goals and the ensuing conversations will no doubt increase your energy for the goal. Perhaps you now have two coaches, the coach and you the coach. Our resources for the journey ahead seemed to have doubled.

Make informed *choices* about coaching - appreciate your learning role, identify what you want and need from coaching. Strong foundations, bedrock to build on.

Discover *readiness* for coaching - are you ready for coaching? Motivation not abdication.

Develop the *values* required by coachees - this is where the energy comes from. What skills do you need to become a successful coachee?

So if it's not about the coach, what is it about?
Possibilities - authenticity, change and emotions.
Perception - curiosity, challenge and questions.
Performance - goals, systems and energy.

Heroic intent

"A man of knowledge had unbending intent."
Castaneda.

I strive to be a body of knowledge where the coachee is concerned. This is neither law or lore, but it does open up some new pathways. A manifesto maybe. If we hold onto intentions then we can make progress. Realize, resolve, determine, aim, purpose, objective, object, goal, target, design, plan, scheme, wish, desire, ambition, idea and aspiration. More overlap with the coaching world where intentions are created.

For all intents and purposes we are in this together. A growing community is signing up...

1   We the undersigned believe it is not about the coach, everyone else thinks it is.
2   We the undersigned recognize that the coachee population is far larger than the coach market.
3   We the undersigned know that this resource is unique, without question.
4   We the undersigned appreciate that coachees need to... make informed choices, discover readiness and develop values associated with coaching.
5   We the undersigned dare to ask 'why aren't there any resources for the other half of the coaching relationship?'

6   We the undersigned have enjoyed three years researching this project, which included over 100 interviews.

7   We the undersigned reached out, unusually our cold calls were gratefully received.

8   We the undersigned suggest that knowledge of process can only get you so far, values is where it is at.

9   We the undersigned wanted to create a compelling narrative, the story personal, practical and poetic.

10   We the undersigned have developed a simple plug and play resource, it is both easy and hard to apply.

11   We the undersigned promote a journey, not a collection of approaches.

12   We the undersigned choose a contemporary versus traditional view, wired.

13   We the undersigned represent both logical and intuitive approaches.

14   We the undersigned reckon there are two suns in the sunset - coach and coachee. We believe in you both.

Heroes and zeroes

Roles and experience are not important here. If you are a hero in the coaching world then I hope you will enjoy this new side-trip. If you are a zero then this is the perfect place to begin.

No more language games, instead of numerous forward slashes and hyphens it makes sense to qualify our language. The coachee, mentee, client, learner, player, student etc. will be titled *coachee*. It's not my favorite word, but it does the job. For coach/mentor etc. we now pronounce you *coach*. Coaching/mentoring/learning etc. will be the realm of *coaching*. The two protagonists are found in business, sport and life. A catch all statement that defines all aspects of *life*. The contexts are slightly different but development and change is central to all these relationships. Whether you are in the boardroom or in the changing room the rules are similar.

Coachee, coach, coaching, life.

Let's aim to be more transformational than transactional. Changing form rather than actions. TransFORMational. TransACTIONal. Operating at a being level more so than a doing level. Two words that will become clearer to you as the text develops. The narrative deals with values more than it does skills. At times these values will be explicit in the text, up front and personal. Sometimes they will be subliminal, operating below the threshold of sensation or consciousness. The values may affect you without you being aware of it. A mix of conscious and unconscious levels are always conducive to learning. As such the narrative has a start, middle and end. Why would you read a book that does not have some kind of conclusion? Coaching relationships often make for compelling stories. Why should this book be any different? Intrigue as to how things start out. Fascination with their developments. Surprise as the plot settles.

As we dive beneath the surface the rewards are greater. As with any deep dive the energy required to do so is also more demanding. Thus the learning points might not always be readily apparent. You may feel confused, bewildered, perplexed or blurred even. A sign that a change is taking place. A narrative where you must fill in your own gaps, reflect and create meaning. Not mine, remember yours are far more powerful. Search for your own meaning, your own words. Disagree if you like, but don't stop exploring. Use this disagreement as a launch pad. Not a place in which to dwell and cast dispersion. You may sense a lack of order, jumbled and chaotic. We occupy this space together, you are not alone. Enjoy the journey, the destination will present itself if and when it is ready to do so.

Potential readers are going to come from different angles. Heroes and zeroes. Consider this example. Which of the following two runners would benefit best from being coached by a more experienced athlete? A) An aspiring 5K runner. B) An experienced marathon runner. The answer is obvious, the 5K runner has so much to learn. They could progress to 10K runs, half marathons and marathons. Plenty of opportunity to learn about nutrition, mental preparation, kit and training etc. There are sometimes smoke and mirrors involved with obvious answers, it is deceptive. As coachee this is an area you could explore. Really there is no difference in who could benefit the most. The scope for the experienced marathon runner might be just as vast, perhaps more subtle in its appearance. Shaving 10 minutes off your marathon personal best might not sound as impressive as the casual runner who has just stepped up to half marathons but I assure you it is all relative.

Subtle changes, precise results. So if you are here with zero experience or that of a hero, you will find your intentions for progress either way. Leaping off the page or buried deep beneath the surface. If you do not find them then you aren't ready, haven't looked hard enough or have used the wrong pair of eyes. Learning is everywhere. That level of precision will of course be important as you progress. Look at sport, so many of the top players and teams are separated by a few seconds, shots or points.

For example, I am pretty confident that everyone who is reading these words is breathing, and has done so for some time, no points on offer for that statement. Time to explore this skill that we take for granted. Place your hand on your stomach and take a deep breath. What happens to your stomach? Many of you will claim that your stomach goes in and if you were to reflect further your shoulders would rise. Think of the physics behind this. You are taking air in yet your body seems to tighten and get smaller.

Actually, many of us breathe the wrong way round. Perhaps our personal image is partly to blame, I for one can see why I would prefer to keep my stomach tight and my manly shoulders and chest to rise. It looks great on the rugby pitch, but find a pair of lungs that has not been exposed to an image conscious society and you will witness something slightly different. Babies, cats and dogs make for good research projects. To access deep breathing your stomach will need to push out and your shoulders relax slightly downwards, thus making space for the incoming air. Not many people would buy a book on breathing, but many of us develop the need when we take up activities like Yoga or playing wind instruments. If you have had this experience then you will already have breathed in this way. I open the window to allow fresh air in, I pause momentarily and I breathe out. Remember subtle changes, precise results.

I am conscious that this journey is an individual one, it is based on my experiences. It has to be, otherwise, we don't have a journey to follow. The following chapters loosely follow the timeline of being a coachee, for me at least. Thus there is a logical strand running throughout. However, the chronology here is not paramount as the skills required to be a successful coachee do not adhere to start and stop signs. Instead, like me you will have a common route with a few side streets to distract, confuse and enlighten you. Enjoy these diversions, remember that you or I will soon end up back on track, whatever that might mean to us.

If you prefer to follow a logical approach where you learn from reality and developing yourself first, then read the chapters in the assigned order. If you prefer a more intuitive approach to learning where you start with your imagination then maybe you will want to read the chapters in an order of your choosing. To ensure I have closed the loop on our learning, the 'It's not about...' questions at the end of each chapter provide a logical summary. You will only find questions here though, embodying our inquiry. Coaching relies on questions, so why would I spoon-feed you with solutions. Can I rely on you to work with these?

To address any potential bias towards my personal journey I have signed up others along the way. This resource is merely a collaboration between myself and hundreds of individuals who have contributed to its research. I have conducted over 100 interviews with Human Resources professionals in the United Kingdom and worked with countless coaches and coachees to create the following chapters. Many of these individuals were 'cold calls', I thank you for your overwhelming interest in the early days when my energy for this resource needed confirming. I have spent my life exploring coaching in sport from international hockey, rugby, mountaineering, triathlons and ultra marathon running. Sometimes active, sometimes the spectator - searching for coachability at every opportunity.

Later in my research I delivered *It's Not About the Coach* workshops. Formally working with coachees in this context was a vital stage of the journey. Discovering your energy for an untapped subject and welcoming the change of focus led us further down our path. Creating momentum when and where it was needed.

Together we have held the question; 'What are the behaviors of a successful coachee?' Thus, providing observations on how one might develop coachability, the ability to be coached. I have taken this information to inform my experience that creates a narrative, personal on the one hand, well referenced on the other. We are proud to share this resource with you and welcome you to our ranks. If you have any feedback we would to love to hear from you, as the research really starts here.

My words, our words, your words, our words. You will sense the narratives at play, personal, pragmatic, sometimes poetic. Like coaching it's a ride, get your thumb out. Enjoy this trip, because it is a trip.

PART 2 – MAPPING THE LANDSCAPE

Lost in the process

Appreciating the process of coaching is one thing but to really be a coachee and demonstrate the values is where true impact can be achieved. You and your coach can quickly establish the process for what you are about to embark on, indeed these local agreements are crucial to your success. Some questions might include...

Why am I being coached?
When and where will you meet?
How long will sessions and the coaching last?
How will the coaching be reviewed?
Are we working in groups or 1:1?
Is it confidential?

A few years ago I began competing in triathlons, an event requiring you to swim, cycle and run over various distances. Like many beginners my swimming was my weakest discipline and I sourced a coach to improve my fortunes. Now imagine if my coach had only agreed the process with me? 'OK as an aspiring tri-athlete you need to be at the pool between 3 - 4pm every Wednesday for the next eight weeks. I will review your progress by filming your swim drills from the poolside and our relationship is 100 per cent confidential. Don't forget your goggles and spare change for the locker. Lets get started, jump in at the deep end and we'll begin.'

You can imagine the impact this would have? Some beginners would be put off for life, some might do OK and some might relish the challenging start. This is on the whole how many coaching relationships start and why many of them do not reach their full potential. Instead, my swim coach did address questions around process and then he began to discuss with me the values that were required to be an effective coachee...

> Be determined to repeat drills time and time again as much of the learning process centers on muscle memory - valuing change.
> Be patient as the purpose of the drill is not always apparent - valuing curiosity.
> Consider practicing the drills between our sessions - valuing energy.
> Use metaphors to anchor the learning and reflect on your success - valuing goals.

I was still in at the deep end, although now I felt as though I had a bit more buoyancy. Over the next couple of weeks my swimming improved dramatically as did my ability to be an effective coachee. I enjoyed the obscure purpose to drills, I practiced hard between sessions and I completed a reflective learning log that I can still picture today. If my coach had not taken this approach then no doubt my swimming would still have improved and maybe I would have kept a log. Maybe is not good enough when two people commit their valuable time to a common cause. In sport this is known as aggregate gains, doing everything in your power to achieve success, from diet, to fitness, to equipment, to sleeping and back again.

Just ask *Daley Thompson* the British decathlete why he trained on Christmas day. His response; he knew that training on Christmas Day would give him the edge over his competitors, something that he could be aware of as a physical and psychological advantage. What if they too trained on Christmas Day? After narrowing, the odds soon widened as *Daley* chose to train twice on Christmas day to ensure his aggregate gain. Perhaps he should have been called twice *Daley Thompson*. This book is an aggregate gain, maybe requiring 20 per cent of your focus during coaching. It does not replace other resources it merely adds to them. Great that the coaches have so many resources available to them. This part of the jigsaw only strengthens the relationship, which is mutually beneficial to all. After professional careers in sport many athletes embark on a coaching career. Not exclusive to ex pros of course. For example, in football there are three coaching levels that one can achieve. Maybe there should be a level for player coachability or this should form the first module in the three pathways.

Coaching is a relationship/collaboration/ space between two people. There are many definitions of coaching, but at its foundation this is all you will find. Two people working together, discussing, listening, questioning, thinking and reflecting. So if this is the case why do we only develop one person in the skills of coaching? As I introduced earlier we only attend to the needs of half of the relationship. It sounds nonsensical, and it is. Consider other aspects of life where relationships, collaboration and space exist, do we work with 50 per cent or 100 per cent of the energy? Think about ballroom dancing and its connections with coaching, one person leads the dance and the other follows. To follow you need to be a competent ballroom dancer. Your partner cannot drag you around the floor just as your coach cannot drag you through the relationship, collaboration or space.

Resources that explore the process of coaching have objectives along the lines of...

An explanation of what *coaching* is.

Checklists to facilitate thinking about what is wanted from *coaching*.

Tools to enable selection of the best *coach*.

Insights to ensure that the benefits of *coaching* are maximized.

Now let's swap the context of coaching for ballroom dancing and we'll see what we get...

An explanation of what *ballroom dancing* is.

Checklists to facilitate thinking about what is wanted from *ballroom dancing*.

Tools to enable selection of the best *dance partner*.

Insights to ensure that the benefits of *ballroom dancing* are maximized.

Now we can really see how nonsensical our obsession with the process is. No wonder in recent years *Strictly Come Dancing* and *Dancing with the Stars* have been such hits on TV. We have enjoyed watching celebrities struggling with such steep learning curves. Yes, achievement of the objectives above will get you prepared and into the dance hall but that is where it stops, and that's where this resource starts. I will let *Ginger Rogers* sum it up for you, "Anything he does, I do backwards and in high heels."

Similarly, why do we often only train interviewers? If we train interviewees we feel like we are cheating our interview process.

If a couple requires marriage guidance would you only send the wife or husband? A couple's success is built on mutual accountability for their relationship, actively collaborating and developing their space.

There are however some green shoots to be observed as society becomes more inclusive. I have worked with organisations to develop the individuals responsible for leading review or appraisal processes. One organisation in particular recognised the need to develop the individuals whose review it is. Remember them? If you do work with both parties the results are fantastic. You transform the conversation, you transform the review process, you transform the individuals who in turn transform the organisation. Just a subtle shift of how we do things with investment to back this up. Incidentally this first organisation to buy into this philosophy was a sporting organisation, where a coaching culture was of course well recognised.

'So how many coachees do you think you have in the organisation?' I was interviewing Simon, a manager in Local Government.' 3,200. We are all coachees, our review system is fundamentally a coaching approach so we all need to develop the skills to become an effective coachee.' I was pleasantly surprised, excited and encouraged by this trip to the Welsh valleys.This is the view that we need to be aware of. Furthermore adapt it, indeed take action.

This resource is just that, a resource. Like many resources this one craves sustainability, provides support in areas that are previously untapped. An irrigation project in the coaching desert. World hunger is perhaps one of our greatest challenges. Yet, we have all the food resources available globally, we just do not distribute them well enough. This resource is a distribution project, spreading our resources from a coach led world to one which is coachee led also. One of the best books on coaching is *Coaching for Performance* by *John Whitmore*. It's on its fourth edition and has sold over half a million copies. In sporting terms the score reads: coaches 500,000 - coachees zero. So we have got a bit of a deficit to make up at half time. Other resources have started the coachee ball rolling, wisely building the stadiums in which we can perform. However, to date these resources still largely explore the process of being a coachee. We know that you are ready to go beyond process and the doing of coaching. Taking us to a being level that considers amongst other things behaviors, authenticity, motivation, attitude, energy and values.

Procession

To date coaching has moved in an orderly fashion, dignitaries and figures leading the procession. Time to shake this up, agitate, provoke, still moving forward and proceeding. Only this time we will take the coachees on the journey with us. Now we can march on, parading all the players. No longer filing one by one, we file two by two.

Whilst we have got lost in the process, some of these factors actually create the opportunity to develop coachability. If we consider for arguments sake three traditional forms of learning in life (University Lectures, Leadership Programs and Coaching) and three parts of the process - (time, ratio of learners and newness of approach) then we get a better understanding of why this book can deliver results.

Time - university lectures that contribute to qualifications can last for three plus years, leadership programs are usually three plus days in duration. Coaching sessions on the other hand are likely to add up to one day. With the clients I work with in a given year it is unlikely that we ever exceed this amount of time for each person. Short sharp sessions dominate. During lectures and leadership programs you have the luxury of time to appreciate how you best learn. With coaching you need to hit the ground running, which this resource aims to facilitate.

Ratio of learners - lectures can exceed 100 people and leadership programs perhaps average about 10 participants a session. Apart from group coaching the bulk of coaching takes place in a one to one learning environment. So the focus here is obvious, the coachee is expected to contribute, learn and develop. In bigger groups the spotlight can be avoided. Even in team sports where group coaching is expected, these conversations often include one to one time.

Newness of approach - coaching is an ancient practice as we have discussed but it is fairly new to the environment within organisations. Lectures and leadership programs have been around far longer so we are able to get a sense of what is expected of us. For coaching there are less expectations for us to draw on and less precedent. The term has been around for much longer in sport yet only recently has it begun to demand more input from the coachee. Nowadays pure coaching skills are out muscling management approaches. There are still anomalies, I might not always end up with a 'coach.' If I go skiing I work with an instructor, mountaineering a guide and baseball a field manager.

In all forms of coaching focused time, working one to one with a fairly new approach means the intensity increases and we need to be on top of our game to make a go of it. University lectures are more relaxed, and leadership programs depending on how they are delivered sit somewhere in the middle. The steeper the learning curve the greater the effort required i.e. the greater the need to develop your values as the learner.

Learning to learn

The concept of learning styles originated in the 1970s and it is commonly believed that most people favor some particular method of interacting with, taking in and processing information. In the mid 70s *Peter Honey* and *Alan Mumford* adapted *David Kolb's* model and developed one of the most widely used systems for assessing preferred learning styles - Activist, Reflector, Theorist and Pragmatist. Another common and widely used approach is *Fleming's* VARK model, which expanded upon earlier *Neuro Linguistic Programming (NLP)*. Learners are described being as Visual, Auditory, Reading (writing) or Kinesthetic (tactile). As with all models there are many variations on a theme.

These and other models are all very useful resources for coachees. Their strength is that they relate to learning as a whole, their weakness therefore is that they are not specific to coaching. Learning styles are unlikely to help you to make informed choices about coaching. They certainly can't be specific about developing values that are required by coachees. They can provide readiness for learning but lack the coaching focus. This book is specific to coaching, but it does not aim to replace learning styles theory, merely being another useful addition. If you are climbing a steep gradient you need specialized equipment. The equipment you used on the lowland hills is similar in design but it will not serve you on mountains at higher altitude and in extreme conditions.

Learning curves

I was nudged in the ribs a couple of times to write this book, not by individuals but by events. It found me. Within organisations talent programs are common initiatives to create tomorrow's leaders and opportunities for succession planning. In sport, academies and scholarships are familiar set ups. I was working with one client to develop 15 coaches who in turn would coach 15 coachees who had just been selected for the talent pool. Both groups were brimming with enthusiasm, wide eyed and expectant. I was drawn to their ambition and quickly sought a resource for the coachees to add to their ever growing binders. I took six books on the subject for a test drive. Sadly none of them took me off the forecourt, all the focus was on the process.

Half way through the program come coaches were bringing stories of overwhelming success. Others weren't, like me they were stuck on the forecourt, looking under cars to find their unwilling coachee and dealing with the learning process more than learning itself. Never fear, I had a binder to fill so I gathered my own resources and put together, a 10-page guide on our intentions. Happy with my contribution I reflected that I was probably not the only one in the world who needed this and has developed their own. I was not sure if we should keep reinventing the wheel. At the end of the program I had worked with 15 world class coaches. The resources for coaches only made it onto the field at half time but it certainly raised everybody's game by the time the final whistle blew.

Around the same time I was watching a TV program where *Austin Healey* a former English, British and Irish Lions rugby player was coaching a youth team that was at the bottom of the table. The learning curve became the story, weight was shed, cigarettes given up and leadership assumed. The team improved, passions rekindled as sport showcased its ability to change lives. 80 per cent of the team's journey was on skills development to improve as a team; scrum technique, lineout options, kicking game and fluid passing. Yet if you delve underneath, time to dive again, you will notice the other 20 per cent. A journey to develop coachability.

One that probably comes before skills' development. The team was blessed with a world class coach, but this does not in turn develop automatic coachability. *Austin's* early skills sessions reverted to creating discipline. Asking for the lads at the back to come forward, to listen, to ask questions, to engage. To be, not do. The captain made great progress diving deep, others are probably still resistant to being coached. A world class coach is not enough, unless that is the coachee is willing to be world class also.

Mapping the hero's journey

My research suggests that coachees go on a journey as they begin to make informed choices about coaching, discover readiness for coaching and develop the values required by coachees.

The map isn't too detailed, that is not necessary. Tracking the journey are three levels of coachability; possibilities, perception and performance. Sitting in these three areas are three sets of values. Thus there are nine areas mapped out...

Consider *Possibilities* Aware
As coachee you will be *considering* all your different possibilities and in doing so *awareness* of yourself and others will increase.
Starting values - authenticity. Middle values - change. End values - emotions.
Challenge *Perception* Adapt
As coachee you will be *challenging* your perception and

adapting accordingly.

Starting values - curiosity. Middle values - challenge. End values - questions.

Change *Performance* Action

As coachee you will be *changing* your performance and taking *action*.

Starting values - goals. Middle values - systems. End values - energy.

Possibilities, perception and performance really define the map and potential journeys. Not much else is needed, this should give you enough to go on. However, if you are looking for another level of detail then the start, middle and end can provide this. For example, I was starting to work with possibilities, finding my feet in the middle ground and finally excelling in this area. A journey within the journey if you like. Then I could move confidently forward to adapting my perception. By combining these areas our map forms a nine point grid. Of course I have populated these nine areas based on my research and personal experience. They will no doubt go some way in describing your journey. Remember the opening pages, hold onto your views of the world. It's not about me, it's about you. Maybe you will create destinations that resonate with your situation or personality.

Like any map, choose to use it your own way. Follow the directions observing landmarks and taking bearings at every turn. Study your intended route, seeking out points of interest, short cuts and day trips. Dig it out when you are lost and need to locate your present position. Spread it across the kitchen table and allow it to inspire you. Rip it up and rely on your internal compass to guide you safely.

Later on you can fold the map up, you know what it is about. The search for the hero has begun and challenges noted. Our intentions will signpost the way, whoever we are. We have mapped the landscape. No chance that we will get lost in the process or follow the procession. On the curve of learning to learn we have found our map.

Introductions are over, but these aren't simple formalities. Our journey has already begun, possibilities flow. The key concepts have already been revealed, perception starting to shift. Now we must visit them formally, allowing performance to shine.

PART 3 - POSSIBILITIES

What's your story?

Possibilities

It's all invented, everything you can and can't do. It's just a story. There are plenty of contributors but you are the author. *Martin Luther King* said, "I have a dream." That was his *narrative*. He didn't say, 'I have a plan.' You know how he assessed his possibilities. Anything is possible. Endless possibilities that you struggle to keep up with. A narrative that is constantly in flow, defining and redefining. The person you are one day is not who you are the next. An ever changing story, frustrating on the one hand exhilarating on the other.

A story that grounds you, takes you to your center, connects with your *soul*. What you really want to achieve deep down. Gentle and relaxing possibilities. Depth, essence and identity. Day dreaming, part of who we are.

Noticing changes in our *body*. Spring in our step as we bound from one possibility to another. Energy shifts, the story floods out. People want to connect with our vision, hanging onto your coat tails and the final chapter of your story.

Our *heart* plays an important role, guiding the narrative. Providing a safe environment in which to operate. Proud, excitable, scared, intuitive. Possibilities emerge. Smiles and laughter. What we know to be true, without quantification.

Our *mind* hangs onto these possibilities. As the narrative plays out it keeps track of your progress. A school of thought. Thoughts graduate. Don't over think, too much logic can kill off your greatest ideas.

Your story takes on its own meaning. Possibilities that fuel your *spirit*. Connecting to other stories seamlessly, morals and moods create harmony. The author and narrative combined, neither is the dominant force. Breathe in, breathe out. Breath.

Chapter I

Authenticity

Primary values

I was in Primary School aged 10 when I realized that authenticity was important to me, although I would have never have called it that then. To me authenticity means recognizing your inner values and demonstrating them externally. Inside out. Skillfully of course, otherwise you might be labeled a maverick.

I could not wait to get into Mr. Sanders' class, the final one of my Primary School apprenticeship. I felt privileged, a feeling that I would not experience again in academia. Like any good coach his portfolio was wide ranging. His book club discussion lives with me today and his surfing guidance brought him into our family circle. Above all he was authentic and appeared to love teaching.

His passion for rugby was infectious, as was his reward for tackling him in training. A *Mars* bar no less, such luxury for one so young. He told me that because I had such a low center of gravity that I would make a great scrum half. I could not believe that someone was taking such an interest in me and that he had given me feedback about something so specific and personal. This was my first position of any sort in life, the fact that it was well thought out made it all the more special. At the schoolboy trials Mr. Sanders was our referee. We were playing at Underhill Park. A great big basin of sports' pitches surrounded by trees that would remind me of the world that *Tolkien* had created. I will never forget the advice he gave me when a scrum was awarded. 'Have a go yourself,' I could not believe it, he was supposed to remain unbiased yet he had recognized the need to get me into the game.

It did not have a fairytale ending as I didn't make the regional team, but I will never forget my first taste of coaching genius. This was the start of my authentic journey, one where I could create outlandish possibilities. His comment would serve me later in life, not necessarily at the back of scrums but in times of equal mayhem.

I remember clearly being in the school assembly hall with Mr. Sanders. He was describing the concept of anachronisms. Being a skillful coach he asked me to come up with an example. I replied, 'it would be like seeing a helicopter in a cave man film.' Not tremendously articulate but it is an example I am happy with 30 or so years later.

Looking at the dictionary and you will find 'a thing belonging or appropriate to a period other than that in which it exists, especially a thing that is conspicuously old-fashioned.' So I wasn't far off all those years ago. More loosely something that doesn't feel right. It might be glaringly obvious, or subtly troubling you. This sense remained with me from that day forward. If something does not seem right, it keeps gnawing away at me. Sometimes it can take years to truly surface.

Journeys have a habit of finishing one moment and starting the next. I moved to the 'big school' and lost touch with my first coach, a few teachers inspired me but nothing to write home about. Fortunately another journey presented itself, the Scouting movement. Like many lessons the negative consequences surfaced before the positive benefits.

We were a few weeks away from my first camp. The highlight of the Scouting world, where other troops came together for a weekend under green canvas. At the end of one of our meetings a patrol leader sat us all down on the dusty floor. Slowly catching our breath from playing games, probably man in a lifeboat or dodge ball. 'We'll be going to the camp come what may. Even if it is under two feet of water the bus will still be leaving Friday night.' So it rained, and rained for most of the following week. I would look out the window from school and worry about the drizzle, the downpours in the morning as we left the house the odd glimpse of sunshine only to be returned quickly into a sodden state. Rugby was canceled, enough to leave me feeling empty but this time I knew it might jeopardize the camp. The patrol leader had said we were going come what may. I do not know why but this felt like an anachronism. It was subtly troubling me. I was valuing authenticity, I was valuing integrity. The bus arrived and we set off despite the rain. I can't remember exactly where, but we turned around. I was disappointed, he had promised. I had smelt an anachronism and it came into being.

Recognizing my values, trust, honesty integrity. What is great about authenticity is that you can recognize any value, anything that is authentic and meaningful to you. I suppose as long as your value is deemed moral or ethical then you are good to go. It was my road map so I could create any possibilities I wanted. I knew the next step, demonstrating my values. As a starting point this means speaking up for your values. Something that I hadn't yet mastered. It would take time.

Rob was our Scout Leader and my role model. I totally looked up to him, and in truth wanted to be like him. Despite the age gap he made me feel like he was treating me as an adult. An equal, with accountability and responsibility. I was the youngest patrol leader in the troop and I never forget the feeling of operating at a level which defied my age. We were all rewarded when my patrol scooped the ultimate prize in the county camping competition. Rob would later go into business with my father, setting up an outdoor activity center. This has been the foundation of my career to date and without Rob's coaching things could have been very different for all of us.

My life revolved around two systems in my early teens, sporting and scouting. Intertwined with nature's systems I had structure, something to hold and aspire to. Our summer camp was one of these marks in the calendar, a one week camp in the same location each year defined by bivouacking. The art of building improvised shelters, usually relying on timber frames and a bracken clad roof. If you were lucky you would be the proud owner of a 'bivi' bag, a bright orange plastic sack that is guaranteed to soak you from the inside out should you need outside in protection from the rain. I can't remember if it was bivouac related or not, but Rob stopped me in my tracks with an approach I had never seen before. One of the newer Scouts came to him with a problem, the content of which is neither relevant nor held in my memory. The Scout asked him a question, expecting an answer, Rob replied, 'what do you think?'

I was not part of the conversation, but I was. Here was a new way of being. I didn't know what it was called or when I first practiced it but I was mesmerized. Something so simple, yet so powerful. The energy shifts straight back to the other person. The question bouncing back like *Pong*, one of the earliest video games. Respecting, empowered and performance enhancing.

Of course schooling did throw up a few lessons of note. I studied Drama, I enjoyed it but wasn't a fantastic actor. Maybe I was too authentic for cameo roles. Out of all our subject choices it was the one that seemed the most creative, fun and well signed up for. My group of friends were all studying it so it was an extension of that, I couldn't miss out. For some reason our teacher Mr. Roberts always used his first name in his title, so it was always Gwyn Roberts the teacher. We would never call him just Gwyn. I suppose he set a precedent for the famous people that I would get to know. There was Lyndon Jones, a year older than me but someone I knew quite well as he lived in the same area so we caught the same bus. His sister Catherine also a Jones (obviously) felt like Gwyn, she needed to add another name to her title. She chose Zeta, from her Grandmother. She too did a bit of drama but was far too talented for our class or our school and the rest is history. A digression in honor of the Jones family, maybe, but I like it. Authenticity it about identity, your name is central to this and if a Gwyn or a Zeta enhances your identity then good for you. Perhaps it will give you a feeling of keeping up with the Jones'.

Back to the ensuing Drama, Gwyn Roberts' first ever lesson with us was genius, a wonderful lesson in authenticity which ironically encourages honesty and would not include someone acting or role playing in life. The scenario; you are a miner supporting a young family, it's the 1980s and the pit had just closed, you are out of a job. You meet the person responsible for the closure in the street, he greets you good morning. How do you react? Remember it is lesson number one so lots of social etiquette is going on, for me at least. We stood around the room, probably starting 'to get into role.' One by one Gwyn Roberts walked around bidding us good morning. I think I was greeted fairly early on. My response was far from authentic, more passive aggressive. A behavior I could make an art form out of, but one I have pretty much managed into submission these days. 'Oh, is it? I hadn't really noticed,' I replied. Head lowered, delivered with irony and a dose of 14 year old aggression. I failed, that was not authentic. My inner was screaming out, yet on the outside I portrayed a completely different character.

Jaimes (with an i) Cooper, he was authentic. His response included swearing, finger waving and near physical violence. Now that is what I was after. Authenticity is contagious, most responses after Jaimes' were closer to his performance than mine. I had failed, yet I hadn't. At least I had the key to unlock my authenticity, now I just had to use it. It wasn't skillful at first, more maverick like. No, it would have been acting, I was all about rules and respecting my elders. When you mix the two (values and demonstration) you are being authentic, providing a demonstration of your values.

I did come up with my own theory. Consider this example, take some global chocolate bars, bite into one of Mr. Sanders' *Mars* bars and enjoy chocolate, light nougat and caramel. Biting into a *Snickers* bar you will enjoy a similar experience. Same, same but different as they say in Asia. One description I found included; 'It consists of peanut nougat topped with roasted peanuts and caramel, enrobed in milk chocolate.' Ahhh, enrobed what a beautiful term, ideal for my favorite out of the two. Experiment number one goes like this. Look at the *Mars* or *Snickers* branding, bite into it and it and 99.9 per cent of the time it will match your expectations exactly.

Knowing the importance of words experiment number two is going to enrobe your bar in a different wrapper or robe. Take both bars and swap their robes. Try to forget or fool yourself that you have done this, not very scientific. Or use your imagination or an unknowing volunteer in the playground to eat chocolate and see what you get. Naked, both bars look pretty similar. They will see a *Mars* and taste a *Snickers* or see a *Snickers* and get a *Mars*. It would not take long to work out what has happened but think of the same experience with people.

I developed an opinion of one of the Assistant Head teachers when he joined our school. He took us for rugby and seemed like one of the good guys, despite being a hard task master. Later he turned out to be someone else entirely. I thought he was a *Mars* bar and then I tasted my first peanut, later on all I could taste was peanuts. Something was not adding up. His values were not being demonstrated. Undoubted compassion for rugby, yet crude interactions with his staff. His whole team left or moved departments under some terms or other within a couple of years of his joining. I couldn't help feeling that his real value set wasn't behind these changes. Maybe they were, so I got it wrong. He was a *Snickers* bar all along, yet I judged him as a *Mars*. Fine maybe his values were to create a new team, but then that would mean that the values he described about his personal life were not authentic. To this day I do not know which chocolate bar he was but I do know the robes were different deep down or in his personal life. When I sniff out these anachronisms I go cold, my personal energy cannot hide this. In the words of *Shakespeare's Hamlet* "This above all: to thine own self be true."

Authentic possibilities

Bodies of knowledge are important to me, just as they are to any coachee. Human or paper I do not mind. Authenticity is not a flash in the pan, it has been around forever. A focus on someone's values is certainly not new. The original Greek meaning of authenticity described 'having auctoritas'. Possessing inherent authority over one's self, and as being the sole source of one's own being.

In Western literature the Danish philosopher Kierkegaard may have begun the search for authenticity. In 1835 he wrote, "The thing is to find a truth which is true for me, to find the idea for which I can live and die." Also focusing on the collective he observed what is nowadays a very real situation, where individuals are lost in the crowd. The system leaving us "Phantom in the public... which is a monstrous nothing." Anonymous, despite our need to associate with the larger group. He also believed that you either are or are not authentic. There is no middle ground and probably describes to this day why there are no continuums of authenticity.

Towards the end of the 1800s *Nietzsche* brings in the concept of power. In the negative sense if you are inauthentic this leads to the weak self. Conversely the authentic self "Needs neither the approbation of his surroundings nor the medals and titles that allegedly attests this power, nor does such a self require the curious pleasures stemming from abusive domination in order to intensify the feeling of power - for it is already intrinsically part of him." Again leaning towards society he noted that powerful and authentic individuals need each other. Furthermore these selfhoods need society and culture as the crucial space within which they create themselves and their environment. Writing in the early twentieth Century *Heidegger* another German philosopher brings in the concepts of objective truth and being. Being that is not abstract to the world around us. More commentary on authentic and inauthentic behavior, leaving it with the individual to be accountable and accept the process as a possibility "Individualization is that authentic being one's self."

Around the same sort of time *Sartre* stated that authenticity requires reflection as well as action. Self awareness being the key component in what gradually becomes an explicit pattern of authenticity. The French Philosopher stresses the explicit nature, somewhat romantically describing the search for authenticity as a "Kind of dreamlike, misty state that cannot fix anything." He encourages us to pursue authentic self creation. Although this time he portrays the search as being undertaken alone by an individual with no meaningful social relationships. Keeping being perpetually in question, but don't try to answer the question of authenticity, don't even raise it. Otherwise we risk being stable and fixed like an object. "If you seek authenticity for authenticity's sake, you are no longer authentic."

Finally we meet *Camus* the last thinker on authenticity, inviting us to live out a rebellious acceptance of our absurd fate. Encouraging us to win authenticity by "An act of lucidity as one makes an act of faith." Encouragingly he recognized that authenticity can never be eliminated and that we must 'obey the flame.' Leaving us to make 'the existential leap' the French Algerian Philosopher also stated that 'the way' (to being authentic) does not exist. Whilst many have mapped out authenticity as one of two paths, good and evil, he argued that it is more personal than that with no ethical rules to follow. Let intuition reign, freedom and spontaneity. Authentic constructive rebellion that is socially viable.

These thinkers get me thinking, leaving me with the ideal that if an individual develops awareness of self (and others) then they can begin to attune their needs to the environment. Thus in coaching our values can define what we both want and need from coaching. Our road map, one that keeps us on track and lets us know when we have ended up on the wrong path. However, sometimes there is a polarization to either the individual's personal agenda or towards the environmental agenda. This can give rise to two behaviors, compliance and defiance.

Compliant in the sense that individuals have learned to suppress unconsciously their natural styles and qualities in an attempt to be what they think others expect of them. This suppression of personal authenticity is learned through experiences of needing to accommodate others in the past. Individuals who show compliant behavior are considered to be steady and reliable – a 'safe pair of hands'.

Defiant in the sense that the individuals behave in a way that implicitly says, 'this is me, so take it or leave it'. There is minimal accommodation of his or her needs to others. Underpinning defiance you might find a fear of failure, or guardedness about admitting to vulnerability, and these unconscious fears are rooted in the individual's past experiences.

As we become more and more authentic then compliance and defiance will surface less often. Soon, you will be able to demonstrate your values skillfully. Allowing the present moment to occur without feeling defiant. Doing what needs to be done without feeling compliant. The polar extremes will give way to vulnerability. Both exploring and showing your strengths or shortcomings. Remember they have to get shared, no demonstration, no authenticity. A coach is great person to share with because so often you are operating in a 'safe' environment. Test your vulnerability out in coaching. You will probably surprise yourself, the possibilities you develop will no doubt be spot on.

The German born spiritual teacher *Eckhart Tolle* really gets to the root of authenticity - surrender. He gives the wonderful example of being in prison. If you are in prison you have to surrender. You have three options, to see out your time, to get parole or escape. Either way you have to surrender, neither option is possible unless you show vulnerability or a good dose of reality. Sometimes we need to hold up both our hands, stick out our underbelly and say 'I am currently struggling with x". Not 'I cannot do x.' It's just your current reality and your experiences. Unless you surrender to your authenticity and coaching you will be kidding yourself that you are invincible. Interestingly the word parole originates from the French for 'voice, spoken word.' The manifestation of authenticity? Surrender to coaching, surrender during coaching.

Moving away from existential thought and polarization *Siddhartha* by *Herman Hesse* is a tempting narrative describing one man's search for authenticity. During the time of Buddha a young boy *Siddhartha* has his whole life mapped out for him. A son of a Brahmin (upper caste society) he sets out on a spiritual journey with his friend *Govinda*. Like many great journeys and stories *Siddhartha* sets out with one outcome in mind but ends up being lured by Capitalist goals. He leads a very worldly life as a trader complete with a lover, yet slowly re-discovers his authentic self as he returns back to asceticism. Experience, participation and learning are at the heart of this journey. His moral compass for a time gets confused and he is no longer demonstrating his values. Yet this can't be sustained, his values soon surface. Authenticity is about finding your sanctuary, as *Hesse* writes, "Within you there is a stillness and a sanctuary to which you can retreat at any time and be yourself."

Contrary to popular belief words are incredibly powerful, yet so is body language. Words are so often overlooked. It is interesting to note that the word *Siddhartha* is made up of two words in the Sanskrit language. Siddha means achieved and artha defines meaning or wealth. Put the two words together and they mean 'he who has found meaning (of existence)' or 'he who has attained his goals.'

Too many people today think they can sustain inauthentic activity, compliance and or defiance. *Siddhartha* shows us that this can't take place. Unless of course one can put up with constant conflict and the physical signs of this fight such as stress, burnout and fatigue. If you are fighting against your values then we can guarantee there is at least one person who is suffering in this relationship. You, guaranteed. Likewise if you want the most from coaching you need to identify and align your conversations to your values. Role playing and acting will not work. Find meaning and attain your goals.

These days I know when I am being authentic when I pay attention to my body. I was working at a client's premises recently, the organisation like many at the time of writing was facing cuts and re-structures. Everyone around me appeared to be in slow motion, walking slowly back from meetings, trundling up to the post room and ambling from desk to desk. I meanwhile was on the balls of my feet, bounding up the stairs. I could sense others noticing me as I noticed them.

I don't feel much different in my work today than when I used to play as a boy. When I was about nine years old my two best friends, brothers Jason and Justin headed off to the States with their lecturing parents. Lecturing as in the profession, not parenting tactic. They came back with the gift of the role playing game *Dungeons and Dragons*. I immersed myself in this fantasy world, setting quests and developing characters. I have come to realize that my work today closely resembles this activity. Try and disturb me from my work and I will react like the young boy who wants to keep playing past his bedtime.

The Dungeon Master (coach) creates the space for Player Characters (coachees) to develop characteristics like strength, charisma and dexterity. I had never really wanted to be a businessman, I would prefer to be a player in a game. Even when work gets serious, I want to enjoy it so that it feels like play. I feel guilty writing this story, I am in my home office listening to music and playing. I surround myself with a community of like minded individuals. Creating elements of a new system, where work and our personal lives are blurred. Work feels like play and play is work. *Yvon Chouinard* founder of outdoor company *Patagonia* lets his people go surfing, "We all needed to have flexi time to surf the waves when they were good."

Exponents of authenticity are all around us. The English singer song writer *Adele* has described her musical style as 'heartbroken soul.' In the interviews and performances that I have seen she remains utterly authentic, preferring to stay at home and BBQ over the summer rather than embarking on a lucrative world tour. Her performance at the 2011 *Brit Awards* was simply magical.

There are mavericks all around us also, look deeper and you will spot authenticity hidden even under Hollywood's lights. For example, demonstrating your values is beautifully portrayed by *Robin Williams* in the film *Dead Poets Society*. Stemming from individuals being attuned to their core values the film captures the enormous commitment that can be gained when one brings their true authentic self to work. Sadly for effect *Williams* was cast out. People often place authentic people in this category when they find their results unexplainable. From English lessons to Mathematics, I love watching *Bud Fox's (Charlie Sheen)* journey of authenticity in *Wall Street*. *Michael Douglas* makes my skin creep in his portrayal of the excessive *Gordon Gekko*. There is also something intriguing about watching *Martin Sheen* playing *Bud's* father. Authentic casting indeed.

Developing clarity on roles in coaching can be helpful, but it is important not to take ourselves too seriously. Have form, yet be formless. In Western thought we pay great attention to the form, our role titles, our private office and company car. This doesn't define you, it deceives you. You haven't defined yourself, you have deceived others. Being authentic leaves these forms behind. Quite frankly it doesn't matter to me, it sounds flippant, but I don't care. 'When you meet the Director remember he can be quite direct and analytical.' I ignored my colleague's advice. I pay more attention as to how he will show up today, in front of me. He is formless, yet I struggle to put his role title and responsibilities to one side.

This is all words, words that are only one letter away from creating worlds. Separated by the letter L, yet sometimes not. Our possibilities limited by the words of others, the worlds of others. I have to make up better and newer possibilities just to keep up with myself. Formless possibilities, now nothing is a problem. "My mouth is dry from the heat of endless possible futures; the sweet promise of tomorrow quenching my thirst. We are nothing." *Timo Mass.* Nothingness. 'So how did your meeting go with the Director? What did you think of him?' My Drama studies resurface. 'Oh fine, we had a really good meeting...' What did I think of him? Nothing. There is nothing to think of. Only my possibilities, which means nothing. My feedback will say more about me than it will him. So there is nothing to share, he is nothing, I am nothing, we are nothing.

As a coachee you are nothing, your coach is nothing. Formless and nothingness, beautifully described by the words attributed to a Samurai Warrior, fourteenth Century Japan. His world...

"I have no parents: I make the heavens and earth my parents.
I have no home: I make awareness my home.
I have no divine power: I make honesty my divine power.
I have no means: I make understanding my means.
I have no magic secrets: I make character my magic secret.
I have no miracles: I make right action my miracles.
I have no friends: I make my mind my friend.
I have no enemy: I make carelessness my enemy.
I have no armor: I make benevolence and righteousness my armor"

Division. Being present. Counterfeits forged no more. Transactions exchanged for transformation. Being existing over doing. The author of your story, not a victim of your ego. In flow, rarely defiant or compliant.

Zen, in the zone, real, principles, personification, clarity, trust, humility, compassion, service, natural, genuine, consciousness, values, community, evolve, meaning, power, depth, sensitivity, choice, aware, knowing, love, change, vulnerable, individual, belief, energy, freedom, nourish, importance, connection. Words. Worlds.

Start with doing and end in being to access this world. Switch another letter, being to begin. Begin with technique and end in practice... Harness personal energy.

Appreciate the seasons of nature and the rhythms of your life. Stand back.

Value defining moments.

Live simply, but be complicated.

Welcome the other into your life, both the stranger and the strange.

Label your ego.

Daily reflection.

Develop a community.

It's OK to be sad. Imagination is more weighty than fact.

Stop, admire, attention and intention.

Be normal in the predominantly mad world.

Access your personal sanctuary.

Allow creativity.

Be present.

It's not about doing

Who are you on the inside?

Who are you on the outside?

What feels right to you?

What are you committed to?

What do you think?

How will you respond?
What's true?
What do you need?
What do you want?
What is the question?
What do you value?
When will you surrender?
What do you want to be a part of?

Chapter 2

Change

Ebb and flow

Like many things in life coaching comes and goes. Sometimes we need to engage with a coach, sometimes we need a break, it's time to withdraw. Sometimes learning will simply come from other sources. I didn't share my next passage of learning with any individual in particular, instead my companion and teacher would be the environment.

I grew up in Swansea, South Wales. Another clue in the name, my hometown is on the coast and in my teenage years I enjoyed fantastic summers down the beach with the family in our semi permanent tent. Just three levels to the beach hierarchy: huts, tents and towels. I was proud that we sat in the middle never looking up or down in envy or pity. At the start of each summer we would spend the whole day constructing our beach home. It was a mark in the season that I would look forward to with great anticipation. Wafts of smelly canvas and gas burners would soon dissipate as the salty sea air took hold. Hours were spent learning to surf, exploring the cliffs and playing in the sand.

The coastline and its inhabitants helped me learn how to change. I would have to learn why to change in later life, but for now I was armed with some basic principles. Like coaching I had to dive deep and this opportunity came when I was 17 and studying Geography. I was working on a project that explored Long Shore Drift (LSD) on Pwll Du Bay, a local beach on the Gower Peninsula.

LSD is a patient continuous approach to change. One that involves progression and suspension. Fundamentally LSD focuses on the manner in which material is moved along a beach, namely pebbles. Pwll Du Bay is a Storm Beach. So called because it is primarily made up of pebbles or shingle. Being more substantial than sand the drift can be graphically represented. Thus on arriving at the bay the shape of the beach could be different to the time before. Its river sometimes underground, sometimes exposed. Large banks of pebbles, high up to the back of the bay or vast swathes of pebbles nudging at the tide line. Of course all beaches are changing in this manner, we just never notice it. The sand beneath our toes being too finite to the human eye. That's sometimes nature's secret, imperceptible change. Unlike some of our very visible human blunders.

With a predominantly South Westerly wind and hundreds of pebble readings later I established the nature of the change. Material, primarily pebbles would be pushed from the South West to the North East on a diagonal angle. Once the energy from the wind had subsided i.e. the wave, the pebble would then be carried directly down under the force of gravity alone. Vertical movement. More simply, pebbles are pushed up from bottom left to top right by the wave (energy), as the wave recedes the pebble would fall downwards roughly vertically (gravity). Thus the beach would have a greater volume of pebbles to the right of the beach as these pebbles move left to right. Larger pebbles would live in the left, as they are harder to move, smaller pebbles hang out on the right.

That is the science, but how would this apply to me and individual change? Well, first things first I didn't want to be a large pebble unable to move. I knew this, but didn't have the gumption to always change, my anchor if you will pardon the pun would come later in the shape of one of Pwll Du's inhabitants. I realized that there are two forces at work - energy and gravity. This is true of all change, an energy from elsewhere and the natural forces of nature. The energy you cannot resist, let it happen, find out what you can and see where it is starting to take you. The second force of nature, well you could let it happen again or you could work with it. By embracing the change, harmony not conflict occurs. The energy might bring shock, anger and resistance. Face the present moment by allowing the change. Maybe one day you will accept it, maybe even agree.

Some of the Spring tides would bring dramatic changes to the bay. Yet the change was always happening, the only variable was the amount of energy. I realized you have got to be constantly scanning the environment for waves that might be coming your way or opportunities to make these waves yourself. The key here is to focus on the external environment. Where the energy might come from, set up your telescope and gaze to your heart's content. You know it is happening constantly but where does the energy source lie right now?

Finally, I liked the idea that the pebble had a bit of a break. Energy move, gravity fall back down. It sounds contradictory to constant change but it is not. Respond to or harness energy to make a change. Chill out and fall back down with nature's support. Some individuals go for the hurricane option. They protect their bay from energy and rarely inject it themselves. Like our family friend who was 30 years in a job, man and boy. Either they slip into complete inertia, fade away and die or one of two things happens. A hurricane will come along and transform their comfortable beach scene. They have made the same amount of changes as someone who constantly changes, just all at once. This force is not destructive, it is creative but difficult to swallow in such amounts. Their job for life has disappeared and they are lost in their once familiar landscape. Unable to travel along the beach, unable to navigate to somewhere else. If the hurricane missed them they inject their own energy. Sometimes controlled, sometimes spontaneous. It leaves visitors to the beach confused or pleased, 'why didn't you do that ages ago, we all knew you weren't happy working there.'

It is one of nature's great demonstrations of how to change. If you look there are many more, because nature has been changing for billions of years. In comparison we mere mortals have been changing for seconds. I remember thinking, surely nature changes too slowly? Yes, by our standards it can sometimes be slow. That is precisely the point, by our standards. This reminded me that we often change too fast and that is why we end up in a mess. Nature changes continuously, evolving and creating seasons. Lots of my friends at the time were changing really quickly only to realize they had to moved too fast. In the wrong direction. Sometimes in the right direction only our pace is too fast. I also knew that nature sometimes changes at a rapid pace, way quicker than even us humans can respond. Volcanic eruptions, hurricanes and earthquakes are not slow.

I applied these principles to some of the biggest changes one makes in life.

My revision timetable was full on, but I had breaks built in. I was constantly on the look out for career ideas, yet I remained patient even when I wasn't coming up with much. I resisted the external pressure to visit every University in the land, one would present itself when it was ready to. I appeared laid back, in reality I moved quickly without fuss. To the point, relaxed, care free and on the right road.

My Geography studies had given me the template for how to change. I was on the beach knowing how, not why. Like I said I would have preferred it the other way round, but it was not meant to be. Maybe it was better that way. Sure the bay had given me some clues, pointers and tips but not the paradigm shift that was needed. My focus was in the wrong place, it wasn't the ground that would serve me, it was the sky. I had appreciated the subtleties of one of nature's systems and the inter connectedness of this system and other ecosystems. I had to mimic one of Mother Nature's inhabitants. I was immediately attracted to the symbiotic relationships that I knew existed as well as the obvious innovative measures. Most of nature's little critters are geniuses in their own right.

In University I read a book about the coast's most famous sky dweller *Jonathan Livingston Seagull* by *Richard Bach*. This is a lovely short tale about a seagull, of course, and the resistance he faces when striving for success, change and authenticity. The storyline is relatively predictable but dive deeper and you will discover wonderful lessons on openness and change. That's just it, so predictable, but that's how the point is made. We know the answer, we know how the story should end but place us as the main character and we behave irrationally missing the obvious opportunities. Like the horror stories where they go out into the woods at night with a poorly working torch and a car that will not start.

Without going into too much detail and spoiling this flight of fancy *Bach* tackles the old adage of time and space. If we can overcome space then all we have left is here. Likewise if we overcome time all we have left is now. We think that when we change we need to be in some distant place in the future, we don't, the here and now is just fine. Maybe that will be the launch pad for the future, maybe it is a suitable goal in itself. Cliché's are, well, so cliché. 'We are going to take each game as it comes,' reeled off by many a sportsperson in many a sport. But, they are spot on when it comes to change, focus on the here and now. Keep your energy in the present, bring closure to your past and release idle energy for future use. Furthermore *Bach* encourages us to appreciate that our physical form "Is nothing more than thought itself." To change we must break these chains of thought, along with the obvious - breaking the chains of our body. We are free to go wherever we want and be who we want to be. So making physical changes as well as cognitive ones. Understand who you really are and practice this, back to authenticity I suppose. Being seems to have cropped up again.

"You will begin to touch heaven, Jonathan, in the moment that you touch perfect speed. And that isn't flying at a thousand miles an hour, or a million, or flying at the speed of light.

Because any number is a limit, and perfection doesn't have limits. Perfect speed, my son, is being there."

Ah you see being wins out again over speed. Notice what is getting your attention, get started and learn by your mistakes. You do not need a fireworks display and fanfare to get started. Just start. Your natural instincts and the laws of nature will be your guide. 'I need to prepare an essay plan before I get started.' Maybe, or you could just describe your ideas to someone else. That way you have started. As soon as it leaps from your thoughts and feelings into the written or spoken word then you have begun. Sometimes the first step is the most difficult. Without that first step, others do not follow. Steps I mean, as well as followers. Sometimes steps do follow, only they are safe ones in a different direction. On a path you know well, your footprints ahead of you, behind you. The spring in your step has gone, toe to heel turn to heal to toe. The heel brake, digging into the ground halting any progress.

Changing possibilities

In her groundbreaking book *Leadership and the New Science,* *Margaret Wheatley* tells the story of how she was listening to the radio, a geologist was being interviewed who specialized in beaches and shorelines. A hurricane was in full flow and the geologist was describing the features of the outer banks of the Eastern Seaboard in the States. Soon the hurricane would pass and he would quickly go to the scene to assess the impact. "What do you expect to find when your go out there?" the interviewer inquired. Disease, disaster and destruction. "I expect," he said calmly, "To find a new beach."

Not everyone will share these beach metaphors. Trapped, without being able to hold possibilities. A perception that is resistant to change, resulting in actions that never change. Steering clear of the new, keeping their distance from coaching. Maybe we need some kind of defining moment, not necessarily life changing but one that shifts our consciousness. A connection to something deeper, creative or spiritual maybe. After all as *Teilhard de Chardin* describes, "We're not human beings that have occasional spiritual experiences. We're spiritual beings that have occasional human experiences."

It wouldn't be long before my world view would change beyond comprehension. Then maybe I would be able to operate in this world of change. For now I was being open to change, allowing my horizons to broaden.

Right and wrong is the territory, but so often these two dynamics can hold people back. There is no right and wrong, indeed these two words do not have any real meaning. Look at what happened when *Adam* and *Eve* visited The Garden of Eden and they encountered the Tree of Knowledge (of good and evil.) *Eve* is persuaded to eat and gives the fruit to *Adam*, who also eats. At this point the two become aware, "To know good and evil," evidenced by an awareness of their naked form. God then finds them, confronts them, and judges them for disobeying. They are expelled from Eden, to keep *Adam* and *Eve* from also partaking of the Tree of Life. There is no good and evil. There is only a tree. Reactions to this situation give it the good and evil label. Ironically it is often our perceived 'knowledge' that allows us to create these descriptions.

Change is change, it is neither good nor bad. It is just change. When you recognize a change, just do exactly that, recognize it. Recognize if you have to that you are experiencing an emotion or thought. One that needs to be taken to the cashier at the till for it has no label. If you are going to give it any label take a leaf out of a squirming politician's book and sit on the fence. Do not strive for good or curse it with bad. Tell your coach it is 'OK'. After all you are only holding onto possibilities. That way you steer clear of negative descriptions and do not get your hopes up with over exuberant ones. I describe all changes as wonderful. Wonderful with a hint of reservation if they are edging towards good. Wonderful with the tongue in my cheek if they threatening to ruin my life.

You know that the only thing constant about change is change itself, so whatever you are experiencing it is unlikely to be a surprise to you. What you are witnessing is not what it is, but what it appears to be. The appearance that you are creating. Like a film, life's situations are being played out in front of you. Like a film, you are its Director, you are its lead character. Coaching privileges these conversations. If you cast judgment upon someone (or something) then you are confusing him or her with who they really are. A false identity that you have just created, one that limits your possibilities. One that can limit their possibilities. Or, to bring things right back at you fundamentally there is no one else. We are always meeting ourselves! Think twice the next time you are giving someone feedback. For the chances are you may as well be stood in front of the mirror. The coach will hold this up for you, how do you look?

I was always going to meet myself. I knew I was going to be a bit of a traveler, someone who would leave the beach and search out new ones. My Mum studied French and German in Europe and Dad hasn't done a day's work for anybody but himself. I always feel like a tourist, half the time I don't know where I am going. The camera doesn't hang from my neck but I seek out the shot. I don't rely on guidebooks to find my way around instead I follow my nose. Stepping off the *Eurostar* in Paris feels no different to life in London, my tourist percentage is upped a little. Another underground train system, Etienne Marcel please mind the gap. Now Swansea is new, a tourist in my home town. A tourist and guide, a coachee and coach. Hold up your umbrella please we can't see you. Wide eyed, up for anything. Take me off the beaten track, let's get lost, go somewhere inappropriate and know how it feels to be local. I feel cool, this place does not phase me, blending in. Vernacular, ordinary and belonging to the group. The tourists now watch me, an inhabitant analyzed for his dress, direction and activity.

Wherever I go next is new, too long in the last place made it feel old. A tourist or scholar looking East will find a wonderful description by Vietnamese master *Thich Nhat Hahn*, of Buddha's enlightenment, an example of someone who is trapped on the beach. Buddha felt as though he was in a prison that had confined his freedom for thousands of years. Ignorance was the jail keeper, metaphorical walls and bars, restrictive like the physical form. Ignorant to the possibility of being open for change. "Because of ignorance, his mind had been obscured, just like the moon and the stars hidden by the storm clouds. Clouded by endless waves of deluded thoughts, the mind had falsely divided reality into subject and object, self and others, existence and non-existence, birth and death, and from these discriminations arose wrong views – the prisons of feeling, craving, grasping, and becoming."

Buddha's suffering only made the walls thicker and the bars stronger, birth, old age, sickness and death. As with coaching all he needed to do was 'seize the jail keeper' and find his true form. If the jail keeper was ignorance all he had to do was reverse this, be open and discover knowledge. Once ignorance was gone the jail keeper was gone, "The jail would disappear and never be rebuilt again." I heard a coach describing his coachee once, as someone who was calling out from their dungeon (consciously and/or subconsciously). By being aware you will spot your own cries. You will offer them to other people and see if they can help you get rid of your jail keeper. It might not be ignorance it could be anything. You have the key, reinvent. Remembrance, there are plenty of things that we have not and will not reveal to others. We accumulate a fair number of these things, weighing us down, gnawing away at us. Never mind our friends and family, there are some things that we won't even reveal to ourselves, if we do they've often signed a secrecy agreement.

Confined in his freedom, like Buddha, freedom is all we strive for. Not a freedom that is way off in the future, freedom that can be accessed in the here and now. Freedom from good and bad. Freedom that could summarize each and every goal that you are about to describe to your coach.

'I want to develop better relationships with my team.'

'What do you want to be free from?' a coach may inquire. Locate the source of this freedom and create a positive opposite.

'I want to spend less time working on tasks with my team.'

'That's what you don't want. Which is great to focus on, and in its own way is a freedom. In order to develop you goal in a positive sense, something that you can be inspired to achieve. What do you want, in freedom terms?' The coach is onto something and will not let go until the change has been realized.

'Well, if I spend less time working on the day to day stuff with my team then I can focus on the strategic priorities of the business.' 'Great you know what you want to be free from, the day to day stuff. And, you know where it can take you, strategic priorities.'

Now that is a recipe for change, all of which revolves around freedom. Subtle yet powerful. You see it all the time, signage is a classic. 'Please do not walk on the grass.' OK that is what we want to be free from, but, where will it take us? 'Please do not walk on the grass. We are currently reseeding this area.' Ah, now I understand. Now you have blocked my childlike urge to walk on the grass. I can see what you want to be free from and I can see where you are headed.

There are many examples of this in practice, a couple of old favorites. If you were to take some flies and trap them in a jar. Do not forget to make some holes in the lid of the jar so that they can breathe, but not too big so that they can escape. For the first few days they will try to escape, only to bang their thorax on the lid. What would happen if you take off the lid after these failed escapes, say three days later? Yup, you've got it. They have given up trying to escape and will not take advantage of the openness you have just so kindly provided.

If you are not keen on herding flies then I doubt you will have the opportunity to try this next experiment as it involves elephants. When elephants are young a Mahout works with, rides, and tends to their big eared friend. The Mahout will often tie them to small trees using a blue rope. At that age these restraints are enough to keep them in the desired spot. Of course as they get older their power increases, thus stronger restraints are required. Normally chains and larger trees. Unable to be any more sophisticated these barriers are often broken. Tap into elephant psychology and you will find their jail keeper. Just take them back to when they were a calf. Find a sapling and a piece of blue rope.

When I experienced redundancy for the second time I was reading *The Tibetan Book of Living and Dying* by Sogyal Rinpoche. This short extract was to become my career path... *Autobiography in Five Chapters*

1) I walk down the street.
   There is a deep hole in the sidewalk.
   I fall in.
   I am lost... I am hopeless.
   It isn't my fault.
   It takes forever to find a way out.
2) I walk down the same street.
   There is a deep hole in the sidewalk.
   I pretend I don't see it.
   I fall in again.
   I can't believe I'm in the same place.
   But it isn't my fault.
   It still takes a long time to get out.
3) I walk down the same street.
   There is a deep hole in the sidewalk
   I see it is there.

I still fall in… it's a habit
My eyes are open
I know where I am
It is my fault
I get out immediately.
4) I walk down the same street.
There is a deep hole in the sidewalk
I walk around it.
5) I walk down another street.

All you really need to do in order to change is two things, two possibilities. Ask yourself questions like, what is getting my attention? What is important to me? In this case it's falling down a hole. Secondly, all you need to do is change. Remember there is no need for elaborate plans. Just change, start, begin, set out. Later on of course you will revisit the opening questions. What's getting your attention now? It might be success or it might be areas to learn from. Either way you will start to let go of one model and grasp another. That is the only time we really experience any problems. We are holding onto models that are no longer current.

Is my office window a portal for change? My gaze lands there too often, it always has done. I am looking for ideas, where shall I go next? Ideas flutter by like leaves caught in the wind, gently flowing and barely noticeable. They are always there, in the soft breeze or stillness. The kids making their way back from school, noisy and present. They never look up, the adults constantly search beyond the pavement, unbending. Both energies share the same path, one attached to the plans the other with none. Led only by the wheels of the scooter and the desire to go somewhere else. Extra curricular activities, a play date or post study snack. Hanging on to handlebars, not plans. They can change as quickly as it takes for their two wheeled vehicle to nosedive into the ground. Tears quickly followed by an intake of breath as they near the playground and rush forward struggling to negotiate the over sized gate. Back and forth between swings and round-abouts, back and forth between plans, swings and roundabouts. Changing and turning on a sixpence.

Unlike her my mind wanders, checking the time, 'isn't she bored of the swings yet?' Like a five year old I try not to get too attached to the plans, bending. Why should it concern me? Do not take things too seriously, after all I consist of about 60% water. Got to be easy to change, water, let it flow in and out. Whoosh it's gone, right through me. Could have got stuck with that one. Quickly dismissed, no time for it settle, I don't even need to bend now. I feel light and present recognizing my surroundings for the first time. I look out the window once more and the view is different. It is the first thing that I need to do and it perhaps my biggest achievement, now I can hear you.

It's not about burying your head in the sand
How can you constantly change?
Where is your energy for change?
How will you stay grounded?
Where will you change (space)?
When will you change (time)?
What is getting your attention right now?
When can you start?
What is keeping you locked up?
What do you want to be free from?
What do you want?
What don't you want?
What street are you going to walk down?

Chapter 3

Emotions

The toughest call

I felt the hole calling me. It has always been there, a numb feeling, space, darkness, falling. When I close my eyes I feel like I am falling, dizzy with nausea. Sometimes in control, sometimes spiraling dangerously out of control. There is no start and end, no left or right. Just an open expanse, a void. At least that is how I describe it, uniquely. It scares me. I look down and sense complete oblivion, losing everything I have. I cannot see the bottom, that doesn't interest me it's the opening, the territory surrounding it that I fear. I feel numb when I think about it and I lose all sense of reality, lost, drifting and out of control. Yet somehow it gives me strength, a bizarre side effect of scaring oneself, feeding on the adrenaline it provides. I have only told one person about this hole, in scant detail. I was trying to impress her, I was trying to get into bed with her. Another short term distraction indicative of these times.

Bell shaped like a remnant of open cast mining. Could it take me quickly or would the slow process continue? Maybe it did take me for sometime, I don't have the capability to reflect objectively. It probably did but I didn't notice. Drink, drugs, cigarettes, music and nightclubs clouded the issue. A different type of LSD. Swapping long term friends with transient new ones offered a way out. Ecstasy not agony. An easy pill to swallow, but it was still bitter. I had no traction, I was slipping towards the edge of the hole. Scrambling to stay away from its edge.

Everyone one was supporting me at this time. Some supported and did their best to know. I doubt they had ever looked down a hole of their own, yet they were still able to prop me up. Knowing looks, nothing said. Enough said. Holding my hand when I couldn't speak, changing the direction of the conversation, using code words to reassure me or simply playing video games with me for hours on end. I preferred this kind of support. It carried me through these dark times. A short term view from pub to pub, club to club.

Others challenged me. This scared me as much as the hole, indeed they outlined what I might find down the hole. They were completely uneducated but that's why they could challenge me. They had no idea what I was doing or how I felt. To them I was an out of line rock star. Rumors of drugs abounded, but it was nothing really. They must have thought everything they said was falling on deaf ears. It wasn't, I remember most of it. Matter of fact like it was being directed towards someone else. I kept hold of it, reflected and moved a bit further away from the hole. It was all possible. They had painted a bleaker blacker picture than I could ever have done so. I kept away and listened. The beats of the club would lift me, camouflage netting over the hole now.

But that is all I did, listen to what was possible. I rarely talked in depth, except to those that supported me. I neither challenged them or myself. 'If you want to talk' they would say. I listened. I never took them up on the offer, but I knew it was a good one and in its own way that soothed the pain. A courteous offer maybe, what would they have done if I had said yes. Could anybody see a way out of the hole? Nobody understood, and they soon forgot. I though lingered which left them confused. 'Have you taken something?' No, something has been taken from me and today is her birthday. Chemical in nature, but not what they were expecting. I could not care less about my distant gaze. Looking out to sea for hours on end. Nothing to see, just thoughts, feelings in the body of a 21 year old. The one year to cherish my age, the one year where only the hole took precedence.

I plainly refused the call to adventure. Even though my world had completely shifted. I was into new territory and listening to possibilities for the rest of my life would not serve me. I was in the unknown. I was too young for this and everyone around me had not made this shift. Many of them still haven't, which I envy. How long will I have to wait until they can finally find me in my new world? By then it will be old. Yet all along I considered my ordeal a gift in itself. I was discovering treasure every day, it was just painful to retrieve. Unbelievably I totally accepted the situation. Never questioning, just dealing with it. In hindsight this probably prevented me from further harm. Grief and sorrow but nothing more, material damage.

Distance grew between my friends, and me, dreamlike. Some relationships that had blossomed in my teenage years stopped in their tracks. I had no choice but to leave them. Cut off to protect myself and save them from my pain. It was too early for them, I hope it is years before they enter my world. Even so I had a new strength, a new pair of eyes with which to see the world. In comparison to them I was superhuman, I had survived. Like all super heroes we do not want this blessing. Superhuman strength may be envied until it is you. Derived from pain it picks up value along the way. Obtained from a place that no one else wants to go. Extending and modifying my origins even further. It can be a physical and/or chemical process, I experimented with both.

So I had refused the call for now. The doctor offered me counseling, I took his sleeping tablets. Another short term measure. Each night for two weeks I would begin crying as I entered the bathroom to brush my teeth. I would hold back the tears and then within 30 minutes I would be sleeping with Princess Valium. No dreams to remember, no nightmares to contain. It was my Mum who would hold me at these moments, but she wasn't here for me now. No one to hold me when the Native American Indians from my childhood nightmares tampered with my brainwaves and sleeping patterns.

'You are having a nightmare.' I came to, in her arms. I couldn't have been more than three years old. Held by her compassion, reassured by her smile.'

How did I get here?' I was on the other side of the room from my bed, shivering on the light blue carpet. Cowboys and Indians' films surfacing at the wrong time.'

Come on, back to bed.' She lifted my tired frame back into my bed. A brief taste of the hole replaced with warmth and safety.

With the call falling on deaf ears I turned to other interests. Some revolving around the yin of a rock and roll lifestyle. The yang around tennis, cycling and running. It didn't matter, I would always win, no one stood in my way. Now the hole had less significance. In its place, boredom, waste, no meaning. Back to staring, blank walls no matter. Seeing and not seeing. Drifting again. My intent had changed. Before I was trying to stay away from something, the hole. Now I just wasn't leaning towards anything in particular. Progress I suppose.

Then I found something, amidst everything that was going on, I found Emma. Not a new discovery, but a timely one. When she first met me aged 13 she said she wanted to marry me. Three years later she likened me to the brother she never had. Now she was my rock, less roll. Always there for me, short notice, no problem. A listener. A gentle questioner. A partner in the park. Some challenge, just enough. Emma had her own hole, one that I tried to support her with. One that I never truly understood or appreciated. How could I? It was a hole like mine but the construct was entirely different. Hers was living, mine was dead. Mine was living, hers was dead also. Seeing the good when everything is bad, hold onto people who are slipping away.

We often like to connect with people who have similar baggage, littered around our park bench like an airport terminal. In truth she was supporting me. She protected me and gave me the strength to fight off my demons, I maybe distracted hers. I wasn't completely converted but she walked a different path with me. I began to talk. Speaking about possibilities. There was no doing between Emma and I, it was being. Complete connection, words, listening, silence and views across the park. How my Mum would have loved them. That is as far as I got. I was on the path but it would take me a few more years to really step up. I was drawn into this one. I had to sketch the next path for myself, working from a blank canvas.

I had been playing out the character Pink, from *Pink Floyd's* album and film *The Wall*. In the words of *Roger Waters* I was 'comfortably numb.' Those who knocked on the door received little reaction at first, inward recognition that was not shared on the outside. Now I was sharing my feelings. With myself initially, a reflection that came naturally. I told Emma about my emotional pain and facts followed. We both knew where it hurt.

"Hello? Is there anybody in there?
Just nod if you can hear me.
Is there anyone at home?
Come on, now,
I hear you're feeling down.
Well I can ease your pain
And get you on your feet again.
Relax.
I need some information first.
Just the basic facts
Can you show me where it hurts?"
Pink Floyd - Comfortably Numb

This is the hardest call I have ever had to make. The police came to my house in Devon. I was a student there, it was Easter and I was just about to return home for the holidays. Graduation was a couple of months away, at 21 years of age I was having the time of my life. All that was about to change. My world slowed down almost to a complete halt. Color drifted from view. Replaced by black and white, scenes played out like a film. Slow motion, quality beginning to fade. An imprint that still doesn't feel like a memory. Out of body, out of my head. A production.

'Stay with him,' the police said. They had asked me to call home. I knew. There was no reason to know, but I knew. It was going to be bad. We had incoming calls only, I didn't even stop to consider why 'home' hadn't called me. I went to a phone box and made the call. I knew. My Aunty answered the phone, I asked for Marjorie. Maybe I wanted to use her name one more time. My Dad came on the line. I have no recollection of what he said. We both broke down, that was our form of communication. I came off the phone and fell into the arms of my house mate.

My Mum had died the day before. She had been ill for a month, but had wanted to keep it from me and my sister for as long as possible. The secret could be kept no longer. I had last spoken to her on Mothers day. Another phone box. She was one of the most caring people I had ever met and she had a smile to light up a whole room.

This is where it all began, my need to explore my emotions at such a young age. The learning curve was steep. The journey to Wales was the beginning of a much longer journey. A never ending one. Uni friends rallied around me to make my trip home as convenient as it could be. Plans changed, plans made. At some point that day I returned home, numb, a different man to the boy that had left.

The temple in which to contemplate my Mum's passing, the power of place, was of course Pwll Du Bay. Sometimes with friends, although mostly alone I would walk the beach. Poignant songs flowing from my *Sony Disc Man*. *Nothing Compares to You*, a common hymn sung in my cathedral. Drift wood and interesting pebbles grabbing my attention and taking me away from the pain. The steep climb from the bay, rising above my monastery. I had gone from one side of the bay to another in an instant, one phone call and I had a completely new niche in which to inhabit.

It has some kind of destination now, both the bay and the story. It will always be a journey though. I often visit the hole, this time with skill precision and control. Only when I am drifting off to sleep or in deep thought. You have to, it cannot be ignored. It can't be filled in either. A journey without my Mum, yet paradoxically one where she is holding my hand all the way. I would never have to walk alone.

Emotional possibilities

Working with your emotions is by no means a new concept, you will find it everywhere you look. It has to feature in coaching. Music for me is incredibly emotive, I have shared the odd lyric in my story but it needs the sound, pitch, melody and harmony to tug at my heart strings. *Jimmy Page* the guitarist with *Led Zeppelin* was pretty adamant that technique was never a feature of his riffs, "I deal in emotions." Buried in the previous sentence was another of my music idols, he was also called Stuart but like Mr. Roberts and Ms Jones he needed more of an identity. *Stuart Goddard* was better known as *Adam Ant*. The movement that he was at the forefront of even had emotional connections, the New Romantics. His look as much as his music is what resonated with me as a teenager. Unique, drama, rebellious, costume. Prince Charming meets the pirates. Like you I could go on, songs that take me right back to that place. Back to that feeling, experienced in my whole body. Just mention 80s music and my physiology changes.

Leaving the London nightclubs, emotions were made famous by *Daniel Goleman* in his work around Emotional Intelligence, which brought to our vocabulary the term EI. For that we should be thankful, but I look to others to appreciate emotions further. *Goleman* for me highlights the importance of emotions and he has done a global job of illuminating this area. Inquiry into how we know, manage and develop our emotions brings greater reward.

Emotions are the sandwich filling. To one side sits our grounded and physical energy, to the other intellectual and creative energy. I refer to these as energy sources - soul, body, *heart*, mind and spirit.

I have recently paid a lot of attention to these energy sources and they are a great five point plan for any coaching conversation. I have tracked my energy over time to create an energy map. Asking questions about my past to ascertain how I had ended up in my current situation. What were the activities in my life and which energy source was I working from? As I drew the map it was obvious that I had a bias to stick to the physical domain often at the expense of my emotions. For example, my physical fitness and security were very important to me. I needed to work with challenges that would bring closure to the past and to create opportunities that would release reserved energy for the future. I would engage in activities that would develop my emotions and/or the emotions of others. This would bring energy into my system or emit energy out of my system into another system. I defined emotions as bonding, relationships, healing and social interactions.

Activities related to how I felt about... beginning my career, family and friends. Inevitably I developed techniques for sharing my emotions with impact and deeper meaning/greater emotional energy. It is all very well having these tools but did they translate into results? Absolutely I stayed well clear of the hole and started to feel whole again.

My next observations were a leap forwards by comparison, a quantum leap to be precise. After reading *Quantum Skills for Coaches* by *Annette Simmons* the icing had just been added to my emotional cake. The challenge is raised immediately as she discusses the differences between emotions and feelings. Until now I had never considered this overlap, of course at times it might just be a case of semantics. Influenced by *Tolle, Simmons* states that an emotion is the body's response to a thought.

Feelings, then, are the key to manifesting your reality. Like physical pain, emotional pain surfaces only to tell that something is wrong. As I have already described the two often go hand in hand. *Simmons* summarizes "Emotions are good signposts but poor navigators." So they act as signposts but do not tell us how to get there. As with any signage perhaps we should not react so quickly, instead we could listen to our emotions. Respond.

Unable to really separate the two, thoughts and emotions are increasingly being classified as the 'body,' a movement that I support. For example, we often refer to a 'school of thought.' How come we do not mention a 'school of feeling?' Perhaps the reference to the body will simplify matters and create greater resonance. We are all aware of the benefits of physical exercise, so *Simmons* is right to point out that we should develop our emotions in the same way we develop our muscles. Thus coaching could be described as a work out, only this time your personal trainer is on hand. Plus, I would suggest that if you look after your physical health then the signals coming from your body can be better understood. Anyone involved will sport will know you have to listen to your body. Anticipating and reading the signs that we emit. Sensitively judging our actions accordingly. Do enough of us know we have to listen to our body for other reasons? Like any good personal trainer *Simmons* presents some emotional workouts that transcend anything I have tried before. For a starter try some simple breathing exercises, you can call it meditation if you want.

Simmons references recent research that shows that there are two different kinds of feelings, slow (stillness and love etc) and fast (rage and jealousy etc). I adhere to her three minute rule. If you are suddenly overcome by rage or jealousy the familiar fight or flight instinct comes into force. This produces a rush of adrenaline that lasts physiologically for approximately three minutes. The feelings themselves are fine as long as we let them go after this three minute deadline. If it lasts for longer it is no longer a release but something psychological. We get stuck in it and sometimes hang onto it forever. The feelings can intensify causing our serotonin levels to decrease by more than 30 per cent, and it takes six hours to replenish these energy levels. Three minutes, versus six hours versus a lifetime. You do the math. Let it go so that it becomes a slow feeling.

We can choose our emotions, more math from *Simmons*, this time an equation...

$$E \text{ (the event)} + R \text{ (our response)} = O \text{ (the outcome)}$$

What happens after the event? Nothing, there is only space. Until we choose to fill that space which in turn leads to the outcome. Choose to respond with fast or slow emotions and you have just increased your odds of developing or decreasing your emotional energy. Referencing *Viktor Frankl, Simmons* encapsulates this scenario, "Between stimulus and response there is a space. In this space lies our freedom to choose our response. In those choices lie our growth and our happiness." Physical choices were taken away in his situation; haircuts were given, clothing provided and personal possessions removed. However, they could not control their attitude. "Choice, not chance, determines your destiny," as *Aristotle* once said.

One thing can come before a response and that's a reaction. Great if we are driving our car at high speeds and need to swerve. Quick reactions. Retort, riposte, backlash, counteraction. Not so helpful if you swerve when another maneuver is more appropriate. Then it might provoke another adverse reaction. Like a chemical reaction two or more substances now act mutually on each other and are changed into different substances. Knee jerk reaction or considered response. You choose.

However, keep half an eye out for the paradox of choice, this occurs when you have too much choice, which serves you just as poorly as having little or no choice. The rise of cafe culture is a good example here. Where we live in London, within a one mile radius there are about 15 places to get a cup of coffee. A mixture of chains and independents ranging from builders tea to café macchiato. Too much choice often leads to no choice.

We do not develop a favorite or any loyalty. Now if there was one or two or three then I am sure we would head out for a decaffeinated experience more often than we do now. *Starbucks* to the left of me, *Starbucks* to the right...

Alice in Wonderland faced some important choices..." When I use a word," Humpty Dumpty said, in rather a scornful tone, "It means just what I choose it to mean, neither more nor less." "The question is," said Alice, "Whether you can make words mean so many different things." "The question is," said Humpty Dumpty, "Which is to be master, that's all."

Sticks and stones will break my bones but names will never hurt me. As coachees we must embrace the music, the music of our emotions. We neglect them at our peril. Emotions could cover our every move, from considering possibilities, challenging perception and changing performance. Emotions are with us every step of the way, sometimes leading up front, sometimes lazing in the background. They define one of the most popular reasons why people seek out coaching in the first place. Primordial in nature; existing from the beginning of time, fundamental to the needs of the masses and present since the earliest stages of our development. Relationships. When two or more people get together, a connection of emotions, meeting of minds and hearts. Ones that are distant, ones that require closeness. Ones with many, ones with few. The culture that is enjoyed between two or more people, developed from the energy within our bodies. Together we share objectives, to be slow, to be fast. Ultimately that is all we have, culture and objectives interconnected, bodies intertwined. Romantic hand holding, sporting pursuit, family ties or corporate success. It matters not, our bodies are all we have. Laying bare, unclothed and uncovered. Laying bare, displaying and calling. Our heart beats. Our mind races. Our body.

Relationships that bob on the surface, emotions in tow.

'I was speaking to...'

'I am meeting...'

'I am having dinner with...'

Relationships that take us deeper, immersed in our emotions. It must be a strange relationship. 'What do you think?'

'How do you feel?'

'I can feel you now...'

Reframe your perception, challenge yourself and adapt. See someone one way. Take action, reframe the situation and view them in new light. As part of one of your coaching goals, choose a relationship that you would like to reframe. A relationship that is stuck, or could be even more effective. Make contact with the person or persons involved. Could be a moving conversation or a simple line dropped in their direction. Share your feelings in the present moment, 'I'd be happier if we met more often.' The relationship is getting your attention. Isn't it? You know what comes next. You start. By when? By now. Learn from your mistakes. Observe the lightness emerging from the shadows. Shaded to vibrant. Moving to and fro. Resistant, now moving.

It's not about schools of thought

What do you listen to?

How do you respond to thought?

What is your body telling you?

How can you let it go?

How will you choose to respond?

How can you re-frame the situation?

"Up, down, turn around

Please don't let me hit the ground

Tonight I think I'll walk alone

I'll find my soul as I go home"
Temptation - New Order

PART 4 – PERCEPTION

How do you know what you know?

Perception

Knowledge and understanding underpins our perceptions. Truth, belief and justification. *Epistemology* is the branch of philosophy which is concerned with the nature and scope (often limitations) of this knowledge. The links between coaching and philosophy are easy to make given that both disciplines rely heavily on questions. Question knowing, how do you know what you know? Epistemology addresses...

What is knowledge?
How is knowledge acquired?
To what extent is it possible for a given subject or entity to be known?

Get away from the busyness, re-charge your batteries, plug in and connect to your *soul*. Maybe there is very little or no knowledge at all. What kind of perceptions exist when you come from an egoless state? New ways of knowing.

Your *body* will aid you in your search for new perceptions and challenging the old. Knowledge might exist with the absence of proof or even evidence. Here you can stretch your legs and test these theories, tracking the truth.

Tug at your *heart* strings for a response. Unknowingly your perception might have developed intuitively. Fall out of love with knowledge if you need to, find it elsewhere. A relationship of belief and truth, two very different things.

Your *mind* is adept at creating perception, sometimes the knowledge it acquires serves us. Sometimes we need to let go, logically. Evaluate people's properties, their intellectual virtues and remain a skeptic. I think, therefore I am.

Knowledge, connections, meaning, morals and innovation. Our *spirit* will attach itself to perception, up above or down below. We enter into it, a world maybe. The sky isn't always blue, sunrise, sunset.

Chapter 4

Curiosity

Same same but different

Academic study has been important to me throughout my life. However, with limited choices on topics and relatively tight marking criteria the opportunity to be curious and reflect is sometimes restricted. Certainly in the world of Geography degrees. So it can be easy to dismiss academia's value. Remember, 'it's the journey, not the destination.' So my studies provided me with the sound foundation from which to be curious and how to reflect, no need for a question though. The ability to read, research and critique. That's just my journey, you will get there in your own way. You will further develop the capacity to think in your own way, as we are all doing constantly.

I missed the boat, well plane when it came to joining my University friends on a round the world backpacking trip. It had been part of my plan but with Mum's passing these plans disintegrated as my priorities changed. My former housemates kept in touch and were there for me, probably knowing my desire to travel was being held back by my grief. I only owned one travel guide, to South East Asia. I remember Lee calling me saying they were on their way there, my curiosity grappled for superiority with my sadness. Lee encouraged me, tempted me, respected my position. He coached me to think about the trip, he coached me and I joined him, Rohan, Helen and Rachel in Kathmandu, Nepal. Lee was a few years older than me, experienced, knowledgeable, cool and funny it was no wonder I was drawn to his company and subsequent guidance. So I had set out on another journey, albeit for two months, long enough to develop new perceptions. Like the planes I was jumping on, my curiosity and need to reflect just took off.

I will never forget landing in Kathmandu. I picked up my now dusty rucksack, chalk all over it to in someway mark its destination. Approaching the exit I was met with mayhem and chaos, hundreds of locals desperate for my business. Broken English, cigarette smoke and big smiles accompanied with moustaches. Tugging at my tight fitting Western clothes, feigning to take my bag and offering everything under the sun. Fighting for my attention, fighting amongst themselves, I did not feel threatened, I never do in Asia, their core is too strong. Overwhelmed, exposed and new. I knew Lee and Rohan would be there to meet me, it was my first time out of Europe so I needed a bit of hand holding. They ushered me through the crowds to our taxi, the business had been secured so he was calm and welcoming. My journey had begun. We met up with the girls, the mountains lingered in the distance and I knew I was in the right place. The new environment ensured I was in the present moment, not looking back and only looking forward to my next adventure. Healing indeed.

Nepal has a great deal to offer; the food, culture and people are a delight. As a country it stands out because of its outstanding mountains, the Himalayas. A few weeks earlier Rachel had her appendix out, so the girls wouldn't be joining us on the trail. Longer treks like Everest Base Camp or the Annapurna Circuit did not fit into our Christmas deadlines. We chose the Annapurna Sanctuary trek that finished at Annapurna Base Camp. It is described as a 14 day trek, but boys being boys we set out to complete it in seven days so we could continue traveling to India as a group.

We spent plenty of time in Kathmandu, catching up, enjoying the local food and getting prepared for our trek. Getting 'templed out,' buying fake designer clothing, pirated music and second hand books. The mountains were always there in the distance, calling me. Our favorite time to gaze at them was at sunset. On our final night we sat on the balcony of our hostel watching the colors shift from blacks and blues, to orange, red and even purple. Complexion changing, softer, closer and even more enticing. Once the show was over we headed off to The Third Eye, by all standards a fairly well do to restaurant that would mark the start of our trek and perhaps even more simpler living arrangements.

We were showed to our table, two feet high, with cushions on the floor for our posteriors. I was reminded of school assembly when we had to sit cross legged on the floor. Rugby and hockey would soon develop my low center of gravity and muscular thighs. I was no longer comfortable sitting on the floor, wishing I had embarked on yoga rather than ball games. Only days into backpacking life I had learnt a new tip. 'If I go down, you go down.' Referring to the agreement to eat the same food, thus if one picks up a dodgy belly so does the other. Lee and I both had the chicken, a break from my already vegetarian diet. The food and well placed cushions were excellent. Back at the hostel at 3am I got another call from Lee. One that spread throughout my entire body in seconds. It was the sound of Lee being sick in the toilet, and I would not be long behind him. For 24 hours we sat, lay and sweated on the concrete toilet floor. Making a break for our bed when a) we had the confidence to do so. Or, b) when my partner in chicken needed his own space for his release. Rohan was invaluable. In the early stages his job was to source more toilet paper, but within 24 hours he was bringing us *Fanta Orange* in an effort to revive our empty bodies. I didn't have to be curious for long to realize that a standard traveling mantra like, 'if I go down, you go down' was deeply flawed. Can you imagine if we had all chosen the chicken?

24 hours later than planned we all travelled to Pokhara the base of the trek, 200 kilometers west of Kathmandu. The town sits on an important ancient trading route between India and China. Nestling up against Lake Phewa Tal, Pokhara in an

incredibly tranquil and still place. On the other hand it can take your breath away, as in no other place do the mountains rise so quickly. Within 30k's, the elevation rises from 1,000 meters to over 7,500 meters, and that is where we were heading. Like my academic study Pokhara was to be my place of preparation. I would later learn the value of preparing before coaching sessions. For now preparation took the form of boat trips on the lake, organizing trekking permits and exploring temples. I was making the transition from the young man who had lost his Mum and had never been outside of Europe to a curious and reflective explorer.

The trek was awesome, the sanctuary itself was not penetrated until 1956, held sacred to the Gurung people as its only inhabitants before the twentieth Century. The mix of ecosystems was wonderful, rhododendron and bamboo forest, culminating in the drier, colder climate typical of the Tibetan Plateau. Following the Modi Khola River we passed through the narrow pass between the peaks of Hiunchuli and Machapuchare (fish tail) and entered the high glacial basin at an altitude of over 4,000 meters. We had arrived late that evening so the following morning was our photo opportunity surrounded by the Annapurna range.

Never before had I reflected like I did that day. To a point where I find it hard to describe what actually happened that morning. A life changing moment? Spiritual? Perhaps. Although I hesitate to describe them in such a way. Remember, it was just a point of time in the journey. That moment cannot be separated from what happened, minutes, hours, days, weeks, months and years before. I never expected more than a quick hike from base camp, photos and the hike back down the valley. Yet we sat in relative silence for over two hours. A few cigarettes shared, knowing looks and nothing else but reflection. The glaciers were in constant movement and constant song. Creaking and groaning all around us. Mini avalanches couldn't even break the stillness. I sat, I contemplated and reflected on what was. Nothing specific, just reflection, still and deep.

For the trekkers our time and space was soon about to change. We had completed the trek in five days, two hours of stillness achieved at least.

Our last day was spent in natural hot springs, earning a well needed wash. The glacial river thundered past. Like being curious and reflecting it would give us a second option. A quick dip in the river followed by a welcome return to the hot springs. Cold and hot, or was it hot and cold? Like the water, reflection and curiosity often work side by side, maybe one comes first and the other second. I had recognised reflection for the first time, perhaps I could now be curious. Maybe, or maybe I could be curious and then reflect. I don't think there is a linear explanation. The only thing that would be linear for the next month would be the road to India. Perhaps one of the best places in the world for my Western palate to develop curiosity and perception.

Varanasi, also commonly known as Benares was an explosion of the senses. Situated on the banks of the River Ganges in the Indian state of Uttar Pradesh, it is regarded as a holy city by Buddhist and Jains, and is the holiest place in the world for Hinduism. It is one of the oldest continuously inhabited cities in the world and probably the oldest in India.

The center of Hindu cosmology was to be my center of curiosity, I was a drop in the Ganges compared to the significance of this place.

Varanasi did not start well. With over one million people a year it might have been one of the most important pilgrimage destinations in the world, but Rohan and I were only after one thing, the infamous Bhang Lassi. The lassi is an innocent, popular and traditional Punjabi yogurt based drink, blended with Indian spices. You can probably guess what the bhang is; mostly cannabis or whatever drugs can be sourced. We were keen, Lee my coach was not. He was noticeably disappointed in us. We had come to such a historic site curious in nothing more than a concoction of drugs. His response was lasting and I soon grasped the importance of Varanasi.

With the bhang leaving my system I got curious about motorbike rickshaws. Just how many Westerners could fit in such a small form of transport? Being curious must be about asking questions and observing. The answer to the assumed question is three Westerners with no bags or two Westerners with five bags. Perfect, we were a group of five Westerners and we had, wait let's see, five bags. Thus the five of us set out in two rickshaws across town, and I bet by Indian standards our passage was positively spacious. After all we had no live produce, not even a single chicken between us. The traffic was a curious wonder of the world. My Western road rules were torn apart. The horn was a vital tool in any vehicle, used about every 20 seconds it was critical for a safe passage. Bhang lassis aside it was like being on acid. It was like watching TV, sit back and enjoy the show. Many travelers comment on the INDIA acronym of 'I'll Never Do It Again.' I was pleased to announce that my curiosity was gaining momentum and 'I Nearly Died In Adoration.'

Away from the roads, backstreets, temples and rooftops lies of course the river. Another journey, this time the must do sunrise boat trip. The Hindus believe that bathing in the Ganges remits sins. Perhaps with little or no religious significance the Ganges is also the scene for 1.4 million or so inhabitants completing their laundry. Look at any photos of Varanasi and you will see wonderful photos of locals bathing in the Ghats with vibrant colored sarees stretched along its banks to dry. So far my curiosity remains within, until I discover the third layer, the one you won't see in the travel books. In fact without curiosity it is the layer that you won't ever see, another third eye. Your mind probably just can't deal with it. In the Americas during the fifteenth Century missionaries recall how locals were unable to see the boats of the conquering Spanish. Having never seen boats on such a scale or in such a context their minds were either unable to comprehend the oncoming fleets or were resistant to seeing the conquistadors arrival.

So finally my curiosity allowed me to experience the third layer to the Ganges, defecation. I had been reading *India: A Wounded Civilization* by VS Naipaul, here he describes, "Indians defecate everywhere. They defecate, mostly, beside the railway tracks. But they also defecate on the beaches; they defecate on the hills; they defecate on the river banks; they defecate on the streets; they never look for cover." Like the Aztec leaders it took me a while to see what was happening. It took me longer to believe what was happening.

It sounds completely understated but towards the end of our trip I would see the signpost to our next destination. The charred body of a man lying face up in the water would indicate evidence of the burning Ghats. Now remember, we had just been visiting the bathing Ghats. Back on land with a 180 degree change in angle Varanasi has nearly 100 Ghats most of which are for bathing, while others are used as cremation sites. Like Annapurna we sat, this time all five of us and witnessed ceremony after ceremony. To the locals it looked like just another job. Wood piled up, body placed on top, ignition. Rumors abound about poorer families having to rely on the burning embers of other ceremonies, as they cannot afford the wood for a pyre. Curious or otherwise, whichever way you look at it, it is a sobering experience for someone not familiar with this practice.

Rachel seemed particularly upset by our observations and it wasn't long before we had moved only a few yards away to witness a wrestling match keenly supported by about a 100 locals, rupee notes waved chaotically in the air as bets were made. I was curious about the ceremony. I was curious about Rachel's response. I was curious about my response. Curiosity comes from the Latin word curiosus, 'careful and diligent,' which is all I was being. An emotion, natural inquisitive behavior to explore, learn and observe. It is our drive to know new things, it fuels science and is observed in the animal kingdom, curiosity wasn't about to kill this cat. My perception was under attack once more but on reflection it is OK to be curious. It was truly bananas in Benares.

Curious perceptions

Tolle talks about how words can separate us. You cannot describe something to somebody, you have to experience it for yourself. You can't describe honey to someone who has never seen it, tasted it or watched a bee at work. They need to experience it for themselves. This presents us with a wee problem. If we take this statement to be true then I cannot describe curiosity for you, or anything else contained in these writings. You need to experience it for yourself. All is not lost, there are other ways. When you experience curiosity you will need to be conscious of it, aware, knowing. Thus we can look back at moments in our lives and if appropriate describe them as reflective experiences and thus we have the feelings and thoughts that are associated with curiosity. Alternatively, we can use these words to encourage consciousness and seek out or spot reflective behavior and activity. This time creating the experience.

No one else could have described curiosity to me, I had to experience it for myself, and it was something that would stay with me forever. The ability to reflect would serve me well in coaching situations, I knew how my perceptions could shift. I could be with a coach yet sitting on that rock, listening to the glacier movement and tilting my head back and fore to take in the Annapurna range.

However, my experience that day would undergo an interesting challenge when I read the following quote. "The only Zen you find on the tops of mountains is the Zen you bring up there," *Robert M Pirsig*. For a while I was devastated, my beloved mountains were not Zen like. That morning at Base Camp had no

Zen qualities whatsoever. My place of power was shattered. Not for long though, indeed it strengthened my perception. Look at the quote again, I had brought that Zen to the mountain and not the other way round. Thus, when you experience something, Zen, reflection or whatever, you have brought that feeling to that time and that space. The Zen is in you, allowed to show itself in such places. Once we suspend the madness all around us it can shine. It can shine in the Himalayas, as you are drifting off to sleep, as you drive, walk, sit or stand. You are a citiZEN. Thus if you experience success in coaching you brought it there. Not the coach, they just created the space for you to excel.

Let's rehash, bhang lassis excluded, *Pirsig's* quote in relation to my time in Varanasi. 'The only shock (Zen) you find on the banks of the Ganges (tops of mountains) is the shock (Zen) you bring (up) there.' Replace the word shock with any emotion and the same sequence is played out time and time again. Now if we apply this quote to being a coachee we end up with an equally helpful statement. Again any word will do, but let's stick with the theme and go for reflection. 'The only reflection (Zen) you find during coaching (on the tops of mountains) is the ability to reflect that (Zen) you bring (up there).' Coaching is reflective, yes in a sense it is, but remember you brought that to your coaching. Sure your coach can encourage a reflective space but he or she cannot always make the horse drink. Now look at the flip side; 'I am not finding coaching very reflective.' Now you know where to look to find this reflection. It is where a lot of reflections are found... mirror, mirror.

I would not expect you or your coach to push for something that is not naturally occurring, like curiosity. If you push someone in a relationship they will push back, violently or subtly, they will always push. If you are closed down then the coaching will have its limitations. If you utilize more control than collaboration with a team then the results are obvious. On the flip side if you are open then you will experience open relationships. If you are authentic you will experience genuine and sincere responses. Use your positive energy to achieve the results that you want, only you can be accountable for that. Think carefully about what you are packing to take up the mountain. Sometimes you will realize what you have forgotten to pack and by then it is probably too late. To develop coachability the contents of your rucksack should be openly shared, contraband will not develop trust in others. Camouflage does have its uses but not on this occasion. What goes around comes around.

For many individuals their mirror is broken, unable or unwanting to reflect and be curious. If you take any of these key developing coachability skills away it can be a house of cards, the whole relationship collapses creating newsworthy reports. Or, the house crumbles and coaching cannot reach its true potential. I have posed questions before that appear to have obvious answers, this too has the obvious and the unlikely. Obviously many people do not reflect, as they are afraid of what they might find, darkness. Many of us keep our curiosity under lock and key, equally afraid of what we might find, lightness. More locks than looks. Our authentic potential hidden along with unpleasant childhood memories. Both rich in what they might provide, one in the past one in the future. Concealed and sheltered, neither of which serve our present state. In the film *Coach Carter* one of the basketball players in the failing team declares his revelation on the court after a roller coaster ride of coaching. Forgetting his previous identity he recognizes everyone should shine, rather than playing small and shrinking. Giving permission to others to do the same, liberating, presence and even saving his life. "Our deepest fear is not that we are inadequate. Our deepest fear is that we are powerful beyond measure. It is our light not our darkness that most frightens us."

If you are truly reflecting and being curious then you need to dive deep. The idea of diving deeper has been a powerful metaphor for me as a coachee ever since. It does not always matter whether you are being successful in your dives as long as you are making the effort to explore the deep sea trenches and those black smokers. It does not even matter if there is no conclusive evidence as to the point of your curiosity. Pay attention to the scuba diving hazard of rising to the surface too quickly, 'the bends.' Take your time to return to the surface.

There is a well held rumor known as the Dark Side of the Rainbow/Dark Side of Oz/The Wizard of Floyd. This refers to the pairing of the 1973 *Pink Floyd* music album *The Dark Side of the Moon* with the visual portion of the 1939 film *The Wizard of Oz*. Allegedly this produces moments where the film and the album appear to match with each other. Band members and others involved in the making of the album state that any relationship between the two works of art is merely a coincidence. An honest statement or one that only fuels curiosity further. Fans have compiled more than one hundred moments of perceived interplay, including further links that occur if the album is repeated through the entire film. As a fan of both visual and audio I was naturally very curious. I watched the first 45 minutes or so of pairing and I was pretty surprised at the 'synchronicities' that I spotted. Some are glaring and some are tenuous. Quantify no, qualify maybe. Sometimes that is enough to agree any journey, learning, to Oz or otherwise.

Reflect on it if you want. Start playing *The Dark Side of the Moon* while watching the film, use the *MGM* lion as the cue. Many suggest the third roar, turn down the volume of the film and see what you can find. For example, *Dorothy* is balancing on the fence whilst "the lyrics read "balanced on the biggest wave."

Similarly there is many a hidden meaning in this book. Some that I have intentionally created, buried and disguised. Some that you will create and discover for yourself. Like the two mediums you will also probably notice a few synchronicities in your own world. If you place enough attention and intention on say a coaching goal then some things will appear just like magic.

Your positive energy will spread, others will sense this and sometimes react in a way that might facilitate your goal. You know how you start thinking of someone, maybe someone you have not heard from for a while or someone you have been meaning to get in touch with. Then they call, out of the blue? Or, out of your well created intentions?

It's not about being the same

What can you hear?

What do you need to experience?

What are you going to take up the mountain?

How much can you fit in?

Why are they doing that?

What is your deepest fear?

What synchronicities do you notice?

Chapter 5

Challenge

Walking out on the games

Interestingly perhaps my greatest achievement, playing hockey for Wales, was in an area where great coaches were scarce. The support of my Mum, Dad and local club members was undoubted. When Mum died I had all the support I could wish for, when I was head and shoulders above everyone else on the hockey pitch nothing came my way. Even as a youngster I recognised the political appointments that had been made at a coaching level. It was a mixed bag, thus my energy was mixed. Empowered to play my own game, lied to about the captaincy. Encouraged to visualize success, asked to play dirty against the English. Recurring dreams and regrets often point back to these times. Aged 14 - 18 I am sure competent coaching could have made all the difference. Incredulous as it now seems I did make the back page of the *Telegraph* newspaper once. The headline read, 'Stuart Haden of Swansea takes the game to England.' The photo sadly depicted Owen Jones our captain taking the game to England! I was wrongly identified but happy to make the back pages. Perhaps I was wrongly identified to hockey.

I continued to play until I was 24 years old. I was lucky enough to be coached over the last two years by Gary, an ex international himself. University studies were over, now I was going to study hockey. However, by then I felt like I had missed my call. Gary had previously coached me when I was about 10 and I held him in the same esteem as Mr. Sanders and Rob. He left to work overseas for eight years and returned to complete another familiar cycle as he went into business with my Dad. That aside he also took up some of the coaching reins at Swansea Hockey

Club. As League and Cup champions of Wales we would play in a European tournament each year, which would see us face the best teams from England, Italy, France and Russia etc.

For the first time I had trust and respect for a hockey coach, it was reciprocal. Like many learning interventions the primary and recency effect is much of what I can remember. Competing in the Czech Republic, after 20 minutes into the first game he called out 'Stuart, stop hiding and get into the game,' it was like he had flicked the light switch, the challenge had been set. The game no longer passed me by and I grew in stature throughout the tournament. Against the English an old Swansea adversary marked me. It was a nice reunion but he just happened to be the best player our small town had every produced. A host of Wales caps and he had just been voted player of the tournament whilst representing the Great Britain squad. We lost the game but the challenge of playing at that level escalated my perception of what I could achieve. In the play off match against the Scottish team Gary coached me through the whole game as we somehow hung on to a 1 - 0 lead in a game that should never have been ours. His coaching took me to a new level. Adding a physicality to my game that was previously absent.

At the following year's tournament in Italy the Welsh Management Team was present as they were coaching our English opponents. I had played OK but not perhaps as well as the previous year. Even so they asked me if I would be interested in being put forward for the squad for the 1998 Commonwealth Games in Malaysia. My perception briefly began to rattle, but the hole now had a new letter at the start, the letter W. I was whole and hockey was just a small piece of the jigsaw. Important and insignificant. I declined as my round the world plane ticket was already booked and I knew my challenges lay elsewhere.

I had played for Wales at all junior levels, over a beer Gary described how keen he was for me to make the senior Welsh team. He was also pretty quick to point out that he knew that the coaching structure in Wales had not and would not support me. No excuses, no one to blame. To make it to the top you need to be prepared to make sacrifices and have outstanding talent. I could have probably scraped home on both counts, but I didn't. Coach or no coach the amateur sport of hockey didn't create the required levels of passion. The challenge was either to great or too small, I couldn't decide. I watched the Games in Australia, beer in hand and a sense of 'what if' going through my mind. I was a backpacker now, no real coaching required.

Challenging perceptions

After I graduated I naturally took on a full time role in the family business. I was a bit confused at first because I recognised the need to challenge. Academia to date had had groomed my supporting skills. Essays and projects that show cased referenced work. I still needed this but I also needed to challenge my team and my clients.

I was running a leadership program and just like any good coach I was open to learning from the group. One of the participants casually left me with a concept that serves me tremendously well as a coachee today. He described how he had been working with a client, one of the banks. His contract had not been continued and he realized in hindsight that he had been too supportive and had not offered enough challenge. Visual in his approach, over coffee he sketched out the support and challenge model for me on the back of a napkin.

Low support and low challenge creates an environment of apathy. Low support and high challenge can be stressful. In the opposite corner sits high support and low challenge that can leave people in their comfort zone. Of course high support and challenge can lead to high performance.

There is also a third dimension to the support and challenge model, incubation. So simple yet so effective. I was using two dimensions as coachee, I was either being supportive or challenging. Both often involved conversing in some ways. Both often failed in some ways.

Add the third leg to my milking stool and I had a more stable foundation. Silence, emptiness, a gap. I reflected on how one of my colleagues would often enter the office somewhat tired. Having learnt to face up to difficult situations I would always greet them and often look to progress their state. I would consciously do this from a supportive place or a challenging one. A two pronged attack depending on what was required. Sometimes it would work, perhaps one in three times it didn't. The victim would either slip from my net or reject the challenge. I learnt to also choose a style that would incubate. On one level I would leave them alone and on another level (as the meaning of the word suggests) I would develop the mood slowly without outward or perceptible signs. This fits with the 'best friend theory.' Your best friends support you when you need a boost, challenge you when you need a kick up the behind and incubate when you need to be left alone. Your enemies also support, challenge and incubate, just at the wrong times.

If I look back to when I lost my Mum of course many people around me would be supportive. I have had to develop my ability to accept challenge, but when it comes I will be thankful at some point. My friends Natasha and Marianna both challenged me about how I was living my life. They probably didn't get the response they deserved at the time but they got the change in behavior it deserved at a later date. As coachee you will be in one of these three spaces at any one time. The key like so many of these things is to be in the right space at the right time and know when to move on.

Look again at nature for examples, her systems are full of support and challenge. When I was growing up we lived in a forest. One day Dad was taking me to see my Nana, affectionately known as little Nana, due to her size. My Dad's Mum was of course big Nana. Neither of them fitted their descriptions independently but together I had made a slight distinction. She lived about three miles away but it was more like six on the road. That was unless we took a cheeky short cut on the disused railway line. Enjoying the bumpy ride, I spotted a forest fire. I love spotting things before others and since that day I have prided myself on this innate skill. We quickly returned home to ensure that all was well at Keepers Cottage.

Every year around Easter I would look forward to the challenging moment in nature, the fire. Sometimes man made I guess and perhaps natural it would serve as a reminder as to how a challenge can nourish. Last year's bracken would be at the heart of the problem and the fire. Two sides to a coin, the problem on one side and the solution on the other. The dried out ferns would block all light on the ground below and suffocate anything attempting to grow. Yet this was the fuel for the fire. It would be over fairly quickly as the bracken combusted with ease and speed. Trees would be scorched but nothing more, animals I hope could hide whilst the fire swept through without creating too much heat. I would be quick to inspect the aftermath, within days green shoots would appear and the supportive acts of nature would take over.

Despite its negative associations I miss those fires and the wonderment of what it creates. Mind you be careful of what you wish for. In 1984 I received a call from my Mum when I was round my friend's house. There had been a fire and both my sister's bedroom and mine had been destroyed along with the garage and utility room. I spent the next few months wearing 1984 Los Angeles Olympic branded clothing and I got my greatest haul of Easter Eggs to date. I doubt I will ever achieve nine again....

Be careful also that you do not aim for a balance between support and challenge. This is one of my 'banned' words. Balance is not necessarily a good thing, prefer harmony or proportion the likes of which you will find in nature. If you are on a tightrope you have two options, balance or falling. *Philippe Petit* walked a tightrope wire between the World Trade Center towers on August 7th, 1974. The book and documentary are referred to as *Man On Wire*. On watching and reading you will find an expert in balance perhaps the only one of his kind. It is for that reason that I encourage you to foster harmony and proportion.

Nancy Klein writes about thinking environments and indirectly the skills of listening. She describes practicing a 5:1 ratio of appreciation (support) to criticism (challenge). Think about this chapter, I hope you will have found five things that resonate with you but maybe there is one area that is of less interest. This is a wonderful little ratio for coachees to explore. So if someone is being supportive with you lets say on roughly five occasions it might be time to ask for or seek out a challenge. This ability to listen is the second part of the formula. Questions and support/challenge would be nothing without this vital component. That is where you will solve the problems that you pose in your open questions or build relationships that will nourish you.

Attention leads to intention. Your attentive listening skills will lead to well formed intentions, which is all you will need to succeed as coachee. This isn't just the domain of the coach. Throw in a few actions that you will commit to and you have your recipe for success. Engage your whole body, particularly your eye contact and use those two ears rather than that one mouth. Look and be interested. Let it all go, using your intuition and logical skills. Give someone a present by being present. Keep your mind as free as possible and don't start thinking of what you want to say or ask next. In *Philippe Petit* we found an expert. In the *Tibetan Book of Living and Dying* we hear more about beginners, "If your mind is empty, it is always ready for anything; it is open to everything. In the beginner's mind there are many possibilities, in the expert's mind there are few." Closely associated with support and challenge is the skill of giving and receiving feedback. The latter being particularly appropriate for coachees. Once you have listened to the support or challenge just hold it as a possibility allowing it to shift your perception if the words are of value. Stay objective, accept it for what it is. 'I am receiving feedback right now.' Don't question or judge, just let it happen, let it wash over you. All you need to do is let time flow and see what value the comments can add. You can use the information like a scientist to either 'prove or disprove a theory.' Remember, respond not react.

The support or challenge message needs to be clear. Hopefully, the sender will do this for you. Often the best way to do this is to separate the support and challenge information. Sometimes people will mix the two up. Support, challenge, support. This would just leave people confused. Yes, you need to know both as long as they are not packaged up as one. 'You are showing up as an excellent coachee, sometimes you don't commit fully to your actions but you seem to have your goals well mapped out.' What message do you take away? Some will get the middle bit to the sandwich, some only the support. If all three comments are valid then clarity needs to exist. If you seek genuine change you will need to know what you want and what you don't want. If your goal is to loose weight you will need to observe when you are doing well, I will stick with this. When you recognize you have strayed off the path, you will know what to move away from.

If you only get one aspect make sure you ask for the other. If for example, you only hear challenging comments there is a danger you will throw the baby out with the bathwater and change things that are working. Let the feedback develop you, not create you. Take a rounded view of their comments. I remember when I produced some marketing material, I sent it to one of my colleagues for feedback. They added plenty of challenging comments but little support. After further discussion I did adhere to some of their suggested changes but not all of them as I risked changing what other people liked also. This doesn't belittle feedback, merely puts it into context.

Cross referencing and getting more than one person's views are therefore important. Remember 'one swallow doesn't make a summer.' For example, I was told once I spoke too quickly during workshops. Within a year someone had told me that my pace was too slow. I was confused momentarily but settling into the 5:1 ratio some people will find me too quick, others spot on and others too slow. All depends on their viewpoint. More precisely it depends on their two viewpoints. Viewpoint number one, people give feedback to others, which are also skills that they demonstrate themselves. For example, I value creativity so I quickly spot it in others and because I value it I will give feedback. You can work out the next scenario. The second viewpoint is where people give feedback to others, which relates to skills that they do not have or want to have. For example, I am not particularly analytical. Again I spot this, not always quickly though. I am likely to offer feedback as I admire these skills. So one person's feedback to you really comes down to them as an individual, what they are competent at and what they are not so competent at.

I received feedback after one of my first panel presentations with a client. The comments came back from the group via my contact. I held them as a possibility and let them shift my perception. Some of my questions to the client included, 'did the whole group think that or was it just one person?' 'Did the you agree with the group?' After all the group were put under a bit of pressure to change so resistance and comments like 'I didn't like sharing in front of the others' were to be expected and somewhat needed for the change. If the client had agreed, thus cross referencing then it would have been something that would have shifted my perception.

'Stuart appeared nervous at the start,' this was a really interesting comment. I very rarely get nervous so it was helpful to hear an alternative view. Was this comment based on the participant's nerves at the time or how nervous they would have felt in my position? I had not received a comment like this before, ever. A few possibilities exist, one as I have described this is more of a reflection of the participant than me. Two, perhaps they were spot on and I was nervous that day. Three, I wasn't nervous but my high energy could have been perceived that way. Given it's one off nature I will confidently sideline the comment, only coming into play if more information supports or challenges this view. That is the trick though, you can't just sideline something you do not like. You have to confidently sideline it but hold the possibility that it might come back on the field of play. That sounds a bit gray but one thing I do know is that someone else cannot accurately assess my situation, in this case how I was feeling. Nerves? Anxiety? High energy? The sender will never know for sure, but they can be a catalyst for the receiver to explore this area.

Receiving comments is vital part of coaching and it is an interesting area given these other factors. If you do receive feedback then great as long as you filter thoroughly. The question that sums up this part of the book is brilliant at cutting right through the feedback fog, 'how do you know what you know?' Many people have had their theory proved and disproved. 'I need to communicate better in groups,' they will confidently state.

'How do you know you need to communicate better in groups?' one might ask.

'It's a feeling I get, I can just tell from peoples reactions...' the vagueness starts.

'My teacher told me I needed to speak up more in class' the ridiculousness of it all begins to dawn.

'And when was that?'' 20 years ago,' a smile on the face as the ego is caught red handed.

At the end of a workshop I was once asked by my co-facilitator for feedback. I had only just joined the organisation, it was late and we were busy making our way back through the hotel maze to our cars. I couldn't offer a response. There was big difference here between couldn't and didn't. Reflecting on my mute moment I realized I should have offered something. I had made the assumption that she was searching for criticism from which to build. I couldn't think of anything constructive but I could have offered her praise.

From that point forward I have made an effort to provide feedback using some of the principles I have described. As coachee it is a great way to gauge your performance. These days I have come full circle to some extent. As I have touched upon how can I possibly second guess how someone is showing up? I can of course guess, but we know how that could end up. Better still I need to keep it objective and focused on myself. We aren't talking about vanity here, we are talking about my experience. At least I have a better chance of being accurate with that one. How could I have responded to my co-facilitator? 'I feel really energized about today, I think there was a lot of innovation and some well presented ideas.' Of course the feedback police would be on my case for not being specific. Here is my specific guess, 'you were really enthusiastic today, you were very innovative and your presentation skills were top notch.' Let's unpick some of this. How can I possibly define whether someone was enthusiastic? I would probably not be too far away. However, they may have described their emotions as eagerness, enjoyment or interest.

Also with this approach keep the feedback in the present moment, avoiding past or future tenses where possible. 'I would have liked...' (past) or 'next time can you...' (future) are not motivational. Keep the time compressed as much as possible, present and in the now.

In an effort to wrap up this minefield, one thing we know for sure when you give and receive feedback the main message relates to your values. For example, if someone observes that you were late or would like you to be earlier you have a great insight of his or her values. Their main message is, 'I value time keeping.' No need to focus on the detail too much, that is where we can get stuck. Strip out the detail and focus on their value. So now you know they value time keeping. It is up to you whether you choose to reflect their value in your own behavior.

The feedback is therefore more revealing about the sender than it is the receiver. Their values, what is important to them, what they like and dislike. Which in a way means the whole concept of giving feedback is directed in the wrong areas. Is the minority view important? Can we ascertain what the majority thinks? Really there is no feedback that we can offer someone else, it will only reflect our view of the world. If you are going to offer a view, make sure people understand it is exactly that. Your view, keep it about yourself and keep it present.

So there you have it. You receive feedback but don't filter it well enough or you base your perception on feedback that hasn't, well, been fed back. With the story I tell here I therefore urge you to make it your own. You can nod your head, accept and practice everything I suggest. Skipping the middle ground, you can contest and rival my views to create your own narrative. Everything will create a response, to what extent is up to you. Your meaning far surpasses my meaning. Eat my feedback so to speak. Do this for yourself yet apply caution when feeding back to others, *Gallagher* and *Ventura* made me laugh when they said, "Never try to teach a pig to sing. It doesn't work, and it only annoys the pig." Really there is only nothingness.

One summer as the hockey season lay fallow, armed with two French maps Gary set us a challenge. I was soon to experience a change that would define my being, it remains with me at the time of writing, burning as brightly now as it did then. This feels slightly odd because I can't perceive a world where this model is any different. Yet I know it will change, if I look deeper perhaps it has already shifted. Sporting history aside my intentions mostly revolve around running these days. Myself, Gary and Chris decided to compete in our first long distance multi stage running event. Having previously competed in 10 kilometer races, half marathons and marathons it was time for us to stretch ourselves beyond our comfort zones. The Tour of Mont Blanc (TMB) is a 163 kilometer/103 mile circumnavigation of the Mont Blanc massif, with over 8,900m/29,200ft of ascent and decent. It is listed as a 7 - 14 day walk that crosses French, Italian and Swiss borders. However, inspired by The Ultra Trail Du Tour Du Mont Blanc (UTMB) race we set out to complete our circuit in just four days.

The awe inspiring route sucked us in, as the race description noted "Meandering through pastures, and creeping up to the glistening glaciers and awesome peak views as it winds over several passes. Throughout this 163 kilometer odyssey, nature puts on a spectacular display." There wouldn't be a lot of beauty associated with the kit we had to carry. One of our biggest decisions to make was how much to take? Clearly with more gear the more flexibility we would have. We agreed on a pack weight of 45lbs/20kgs, allowing us to camp or stay at mountain refuges. However, it was this extra weight that would be one of our biggest undoings.

Setting out from the Chamonix valley day one was a 44 kilometer breeze. In fine weather and on fresh legs we enjoyed fantastic views of Mont Blanc standing tall at 4,810 meters/15,781 feet. We began day two and the 28 kilometer leg to Courmayer, Italy in fine fettle. However, after lunch we started to understand the magnitude of what we were attempting. The last 12 kilometers seemed to go on forever. As the *Stone Roses* once sang "The pack on my back is aching." Our visit to Italy would see our trip take a significant turn. Chris would retire with a sore knee. Little did we know he would spend the next two days in and out of hospital with an unconnected ailment; infected blisters. Despite this setback to our morale Gary and I raced on, buoyed by having discarded some kit. We knocked off the brutal 800m ascent from Courmayer and were rewarded with 11 kilometers of grassy ridge running. The 670m climb up the Grand Col Ferrat at 2,537meters marked the highest point on the course. However, the Swiss border will only be remembered for my lowest point. I was both physically and mentally exhausted. Combined with rain and dwindling daylight we opted to stay in a refuge 5 kilometers short of our scheduled route.

Fatigue is deceptive; a few minutes after sitting down, a shower or a hearty meal and one already feels a million times better. Most of us competitive folk soon forget the pain we were recently suffering. Now faced with a 46 kilometers finish, the four day cut off point was clearly not on our radar. After lunch my partner in pain announced he too was retiring due to painful blisters. We exchanged maps and money. For about 30 seconds I set off on my own to finish the event. Not known for his quitting we were soon back up to a pair.

We have a saying between us 'never get overtaken on the hill.' As we descended near the Argentiere glacier at the head of the Chamonix valley a family of four overtook us. Not in a car, not on bikes but yes strolling. The writing was on the wall, or at least on the wall of a hotel. I will never forget gorging out on those pommes frites and beer. With no regrets we reflected on our first glimpse of the ultra marathon world. One that we didn't quite live up to. But we knew we would be back to explore this world with improved fitness and increased experience. I don't think I had ever been so up for the challenge in my whole life. How can people complete this event? Can I be a part of this? Have I finally found the type of activity that I love?

It was on day three during the descent of the Grand Col Ferrat that marked the change. I began to make the connections from running to other aspects of life. My body and brain were overwhelmed with emitting messages of pain. But I asked myself; does pain really exist? Yes, clearly in a physical sense, but what about the cognitive? Is it possible on the one hand to allow these messages and on the other to block them out? Just as your boss might frustrate you with their controlling nature, is it possible to accept this and move on? My conclusion? Yes, I believe we do have this choice. We can manage this 'pain' in the moment using only our cognitive ability, i.e. our thoughts. Although success may be achieved on this level, ultimately you are only managing the challenge as opposed to shifting it.

My strategy to deal with the pain lasted and worked for 5 kilometers but in order to progress my state physical action was required. In the Swiss drizzle I let Gary know that 'this is the hardest thing I have ever done.' Being the stronger team member he made two crucial decisions that would lead to important shifts in the pain. He took a rain soaked baguette and created an edible snack and he spotted a refuge on the map that would now be our overnight destination. It is these types of physical changes that can improve our emotional state. I was thinking more positively and I was feeling better. We can objectively feedback to our boss as to how we react to their controlling nature. We can ask for a change, yet remain open to a compromise. On one level we can ask for something new from them - 'can you give me more responsibility?' And, on another level we can commit to a compromise - 'I'll update you with my progress more than I do currently.'

I've heard long distance runners preaching the Buddhist mantra of 'pain is inevitable, suffering is optional.' In our relationships with others it is inevitable we will experience pain. But suffering is optional. Adopting a physical or cognitive change can lead to an emotional change, i.e. how we feel. It is a simple scientific formula that can be applied on your next run or during a one to one with your boss. My openness to change reminded me that there is no pain; consider managing your feelings using your thoughts alone. Consider changing your feelings and thoughts by introducing a new physical action, it might only take small steps to achieve a big difference, use your logical and/or intuitive skills to recognize the result. In doing so you will be able to both celebrate the challenge and reinforce your new emotional state and you always have a choice as to how you feel and think. I allowed the change to surface at a time of intense fatigue, maybe I had no other option. I have to allow this change to develop in my life and when being coached as the rewards are immeasurable.

I returned to the Alps with three years of challenges under my rucksack belt. I strolled around the first two days conserving my energy in the heat. Unable to contain my energy any longer on day three I put in my longest ultra running day to date, starting at 6am and finishing at 10pm. Only halted by a severe storm that was raging up the Chamonix valley. Having well and truly 'broken the back of it' I was enjoying a beer back at base camp in the afternoon sun on day four. The difference in me was unrecognizable. At no point in the four days did I experience any pain. It was a tough challenge of course, but the changes I had made to my training, equipment and mental approach ensured a rapid ascent and decent.

It's not about support

What supports you?

What challenges you?

What can you leave alone?

Where can you find harmony?

What are you listening out for?

What is the message?

What does this say about them?

What exists?

What action can I take?

Chapter 6

Questions

Downside, upside down

If bodies of knowledge had served me to date then it was time to tackle the greatest body I could think of, the world itself. To date I hadn't been getting the answers I was looking for. Or, maybe I was unable to ask the questions that would turn my world upside down. I would soon create my own body of knowledge, not just the inherent learning but 635 journal entries. Like most students the round the world trip was just an extension of University. My Nepal and India trips had obviously added the necessary fuel to the fire. With the loss of my Mum it took me three years to pluck up the courage to travel. I had been asking the pros and cons questions for too long, it was time to land in New York with my friend Andy.

I was full of questions and that is what I needed. I didn't have the answers yet, but I was patient. Ideas flowed about travel and life, and as long as I remained in that state as well as the United States I was happy. Coming from South Wales the USA obviously slapped me around the face a few times and showed me how man made it could be. We walked around Manhattan with our backpacks on, the tall buildings creating a feeling I was familiar with. Being at the foot of a mountain, the cold air whistling through the valley and a sense of foreboding as the peaks loom above creating shadow and healthy anxiety below. Yet man was all around, staring at the out of place Welsh lads who had offset the *Gucci* and *Fendi* handbags with their battered 75-liter rucksacks. We sat for hours in our hotel room just off Times Square looking down on the crowds going about their business. These days I have got family in New York and any time I visit I always pay a quick homage to the Commonwealth Hotel. It was where I first learnt to work with questions, not answers.

The question was developing as we traveled to Washington, only in truth to see the White House. Another man made construction in the absurdly man made business of politics. Andy sketched the building beautifully but our travels were driven on, literally. We stepped onto the silver and grey machine that is the *Greyhound* bus and got off five days later in Dallas. Nobody seemed to know us as we actively tried to know them, I was anonymous for the first time ever. 'You're from Wales? I am really sorry to hear about your Princess.' 'Wales eh? What part of Scotland is that?' If there is an answer I was close to finding it in two days flat. Neglecting most things since Washington our pilgrimage took us to Flagstaff, the access point for the Grand Canyon. The next few days we were spent driving, trekking, climbing and walking this wonderful feature. Still anonymous but now with comfort. Questions surfaced about beauty, natural phenomenon and our man made constructions.

From our travels so far we were well placed to answer these. Yet the next day would give us the best comparison possible. Las Vegas, from nature's wonder to man's. The answer, well like I said it's not the answer that counts it's the questions. If I were to provide one then I it would be this. Vegas was amazing, I couldn't believe how one day we were in awe of nature and the next man. It would appear that nature's beauty is long term, sustainable and calming. Whereas Vegas was the opposite, three days was enough. Unfortunately our next stop wasn't Yosemite National Park it was Los Angeles.

We had only spent two weeks in the USA and we were about to spend four weeks in Fiji, tiny and poles apart by comparison. The Fijian highlight was traveling to Tavenui the third biggest island. It was here we stayed at 'Waisale's Place,' simple tents by the sea and a 'bure,' the Fijian word for a wood and straw hut in which to cook and hang out. It was a question of living a simple existence, that was the question. Eating, drinking, snorkeling, rugby, running and making friends. I would watch Waisale go fishing, he would come back and casually drop off some of his catch with us. Or he would leave us fruit as he was making his way home. You could hitch a ride on the dirt road to be dropped off at the waterfalls or local village. We were on Fiji time, question was could these Western junkies handle it. It had to be an overwhelming yes, but it is a question I still ask now.

I spent over a year living and working in New Zealand and Australia. Within days questions about my independence surfaced. Andy had his own burning question, he asked me if I would mind whether he went home for Christmas. We had only been away for three months yet he had answered his question about independence and I was about to answer mine. 'No probs,' I replied. I think that resonated with him after all my Dad used to call him 'Andy no probs' as he was potentially the most laid back person I have ever met. We had travelled in New Zealand with three great lads from Sweden, aka Team Sweden, so he knew I was in safe hands for a Christmas in Sydney.

To date there had always been a system to back up my relative independence though. There was Dad, the family business, friends or if I needed it a hand out from the Government in the shape of a dole out. In Australia some of those systems existed yet they were remote to the point that they offered little or no support. In the New Year I moved into a flat and picked up a job. My independence was starting to take off. Andy returned, he took a room at the flat, got a job at my work, met an Australian girl, fell madly in love, fell madly out of love, returned home and I haven't seen him since.

Speaking of not seeing people since, my friend Trish arrived from the UK, she was best friends with my first serious girlfriend. Like Andy she took a room at the flat and she now became my new traveling partner. After six months of working in Sydney we had enough money to start traveling. We made a great couple of stops up the East Coast, Byron Bay and Fraser Island in particular. When we got to Airlie Beach we chose different boat trips, I preferred a catamaran trip that camped overnight versus a three day voyage that would have seen me united with my wobbly sea legs. We came back with a different group of friends, and no stories of sea sickness. I was to head to Magnetic Island a few days early and meet Trish there. I met a tantalizing group of girls on the ferry and haven't seen Trish since. The island did not have the power to bring us together, we were poles apart. I was seeking out answers to my independence question and both Andy and Trish were important partners in that answer finding process. Andy gave me the energy to travel and Trish instilled the confidence in me to go it alone. Thank you both.

I overstayed my Australian visa by a month and I arrived in Indonesia without the required onward ticket. I escaped my trials with passport control in both countries and quickly reverted to local culture in Asia as a 10 dollar bribe seemed to do the trick. Malaysia and Thailand were soon to follow but it wasn't until I arrived in Cambodia that questions would invade my thinking. It is somewhat sad that a history of genocide and war was required to shake me out of my traveling stupor. Inspiring trips to Angkor Wat the great Khumer temple complex and sobering ones to the Killing Fields, the sites where large numbers of people were killed and buried by the Khumer Rouge regime. Crumbling architecture overtaken by nature and open holes littered with bones and clothing. Questions of revenge, pity, remorse. 'Why aren't these people angry? How can they accept what has happened? How come there is no obvious reaction to Dan the American who is traveling with us?'

Maybe there should be a saying; in Asia there is never one question, in Asia there are many questions. I will coin the phrase if you like but that was certainly my experience. Perhaps this is why the East is deemed to be a place of such spiritual meaning because they stop to formulate and hold questions. Ones that have the ability to shift our perception. How many questions were being asked on the streets on Manhattan that day? Of course the grass is always greener, and people get stuck in the 'Karma Cola' trap. The West looks to the East for Karma, the East looks to the West for Cola. Both societies asking questions about what they don't have.

I can't help thinking there is a dominant part of me that feels so at home in Asia. Perhaps that should be the question. Maybe one of reincarnation, a meta question that I am scared to even mutter. I return to the writings of *Pirsig*, he said "There's a theoretic component of man's existence which is primarily Western and an esthetic component of man's existence which is seen more strongly in the Orient and that these never seem to meet." I think he's right, but I think they can meet and be in harmony. You would end up with Carma or Kola but that would work.

Questioning perception

For two years I held many questions, beauty, simplicity, independence and acceptance. Indeed I attained many answers. I take this into my coaching now. I like to think of this as counter culture. Society is a 'tellaholic' one, so often rewarded for the answer. Traditional education is an obvious example of this. Yet coachees flourish when they can work with questions not answers. They flourish when they enter into dialogue searching for the question and then paradoxically into answers. Dialogue - such an under or miss-used term, *Paulo Freire* in his classic text Pedagogy of the Oppressed describes dialogue as "The encounter among men to 'name' the world." In my context here to name the question, goal, vision, desired state etc. He went on to boldly state that dialogue is a "Fundamental precondition for true humanization." It is the question that really drives us, the answers are there and they will find you if you want them to.

Discourse also. Debate, discussion, conversation, talk,

conference, powwow, confab, utterances. Speak or write author-itatively about a topic, maybe coming back to authenticity. Reasoning, running to and fro. The topic of roles is an ideal one for discourse. Is there a need to appreciate your role with clarity? Of course too much clarity could result in stuckness, stuck to a role and unable to flex. So let's enter this discussion with two poles - form and formless which we touched upon earlier. As sure as I am that you are either standing up, sitting down or lying down then I am sure that there are three roles you might employ.

Team role, leadership role and coaching role. Search for clarity, the form, but remain open, formless. This is all there is, these three roles, you will be camping out in all three but sometimes you will have stronger foundations in one or more of these roles than others.Teams are like water, they are ubiquitous. Sports teams flowing like rivers, work teams forming like glaciers, community teams rising like the tide and family teams filling like lakes. If water covers 70.9 per cent of the Earth's surface, then so do teams. If water is vital for all known forms of life, then so are teams. Feel free to explore your team role in whatever way suits you. I will throw in two values that I have seen time and time again in effective teams. Choice and play...

Today's society thrives on the idea of choice. The options for what to eat or where to travel have never been so vast or readily available, and they are often rapidly attained at the touch of a button. Teams need to reflect society by meeting the ongoing needs and wants of participants. I believe there is always an opportunity to create a space that provides this choice – partic-ipant led and highly interactive. A space where individuals can choose tasks relevant to them, decide on the best methods or explore different ways to feedback on their success.

If participants choose then options are provided for a tailor made, bespoke, individual yet collective experience. The first rule of change is to involve those affected which is precisely what this team approach offers. It is impossible to expect any team to function if participants do not have the opportunity to personally interact with it. After all when was the last time you saw a river flowing in a straight line?

Learning will become accelerated and deeper, thus generating greater: accountability, resonance, authenticity and challenge. Ownership for learning and the team environment will increase. Variety in both content and the people that they interact with. Experiences created that make the team memorable and therefore altering current perspectives. Competition and challenge arising from the tasks and newly forming groups. We know that there are always at least two choices. Two paths to take. One is easy, and that's its only reward.

Next let's look at something we all love to do in many different forms, play. All play will have some kind of meaning, even if it doesn't look like it at the time. Teams and roles need to resemble play. Play can create a unique environment, one that has serious implications yet practiced in an inspiring way, tapping into the energy and creativity of participants. The following game traits are important in any team. The goal of the team is a specific outcome that participants will work to achieve in groups, this embodies team work. Rules, boundaries and limitations will exist creating obstacles and challenges. An open feedback system will inform participants on how close they are to achieving their goal. Finally, voluntary participation requires that everyone who is part of this team knowingly and willingly accepts the goal, the limitations and the feedback.

We are playing all the time, in and out of work whether we admit it or not. *Jane McGonigal*, a guru in the gaming industry quotes a recent major survey of high level executives, including chief executive officers, chief financial officers, and presidents and found that, "70 per cent of them regularly play casual computer games while working." If the team has game like qualities then we will roll the dice to see who goes first.

Otherwise it will be game over before we even start.

Recently I was presented with anecdotal evidence that this approach to teams works. In typical fashion I was shown where it wasn't working, choice and play had left the building. One of my clients asked me to come and spend some time with their team so that I could support them in the roll out of their strategy as a major project was coming to fruition. The manager and team had worked for 18 months on a particularly innovative project. They thought they had unlocked one of best new ideas in the charitable sector. I had heard how hard they had worked and the enthusiasm that fueled their commitment. Long hours clocked, other projects shelved and personal lives put on hold.

However, in the time it took to schedule my visit the CEO had pulled the plug on the project. No consultation, only one bottom line taken into consideration. The team and my subsequent brief had shifted dramatically. These highly creative individuals were in the doldrums, no energy, only deflation. Having met many of the team before I began with some coaching questions.

'How many of you turn up for work later than you did when the project was live?' Everyone in the room put a hand in the air.

I continued 'and how many of you now go home early?' Again a unanimous and honest raising of hands.

I concluded, 'How many of you are more likely to break company policy. For example, fiddle your expenses?' I wasn't waiting for an answer, just knowing looks and smiles before setting out on the day's agenda. I had broken down the barriers, as a team they were somewhat broken. Now we could spend time rebuilding.

These situations aside if you have chosen what role you and others are going to play in a team you can now turn your attention to the leadership role that we have all signed up for whether we like it or not. Leadership does not reside with certain individuals it is needed at all levels. Time to act natural, let the inside show on the outside. The earth is a very small part of the cosmos and we need look no further for our leadership inspiration. If earth's history is expressed as a 24 hour clock then homo sapiens are 3.1 seconds old. The dinosaurs arrived at 22.46, mammals at 22.49 and birds 23.14, even our earliest ancestors (common ape humans) are only three minutes old. Therefore we have so much to learn from our environment and its inhabitants. Yet when it comes to leadership development we ignore nature as our inspiration. Explore what lessons you can learn from nature in order to be a more effective leader.

"It's about consulting the natural world for advice," says *Janine Benyus*, author of *Biomimicry: Innovation Inspired by Nature*. "We find the champion adaptors for a particular function; then we abstract that design principle and apply it." Pump rotors inspired by the shape of a lily, sticky tape based on a gecko's foot, computer display screens that mimic butterflies' wings, amphitheaters based on an insect's cooling system, a hygienic surface thanks to shark skin and a Japanese bullet train with a kingfisher's nose. Biomimicry for leadership. Authentic leadership.

The word nature is derived from the Latin word natura; or 'essential qualities, innate disposition.' This implies a distinction between the natural and the artificial. Artificial being understood as that which has been brought into being by a human consciousness. Thus you could say humans are an artificial element, which is quite a disturbing thought. Either way we know that human advancement (industrial, technological etc.) has created a disconnect from nature. A disconnect that doesn't exist with communities that are reliant on nature, a disconnect that was rarely experienced by our ancestors or the 50 per cent of the world population who still work on the land today.

Your leadership style, like nature could come down to two concepts - systems and inhabitants. Consider how you could appreciate the subtleties of systems, our inter connectedness. Think about mimicking nature's inhabitants and being part of symbiotic relationships and innovation. This all might sound a bit revolutionary, but I prefer to describe it as evolutionary. Naturally.

Teams and leadership offer perhaps the two most obvious forms to consider. The third is right in front of you - coaching. Now at this point my first angle of attack would be the role of the coachee. Seeing as we have covered that move we are left with the role of the coach. In fact we have got the coaching role covered here by default because we know developing as a coachee will ensure you develop as a coach also. Like our ballroom dancers the two go hand in hand.

You will be able to shift conversations from talking about what we do to the deeper levels of what we think and feel, encourage others to see the world from a different perspective and to create new and exciting possibilities. By coaching you will increase self awareness and self exploration about our interests and how these relate to great performance and our development needs.

On a broader level a coaching culture may emerge, opening up the possibility of a future that is not constrained by the past, or what the past tells you is achievable. Coaching is about 'unlearning' old habits and outdated beliefs. The key role of a coachee is to create a new future, in which individuals go beyond what is normally deemed possible. Feeding back into the team and leadership forms individuals who can learn to see how they are currently operating in life, and what stops them from achieving the goals and results they hold as being outside their comfort zone. A coaching role enables someone to gain access to seeing another perspective, which is wider, and more far reaching than the perspective they usually have about themselves, their career and how to make an impact.

The purpose of working with a coach ultimately is to hold questions and create a new freedom. One in which individuals are able to act on a new idea, to take on a new challenge and to find a new courage to experiment and even fail. In fact, a new freedom to be fully self-expressed. Through the process individuals commit to the actions and next steps they need to take to turn their vision into a reality. Therefore you will develop increased accountability and a delegated model of managing.

We hold the question, nothing more nothing less. We search out answers and we wait for them to arrive. Playful. That is life, and since coaching is part of life then by definition it's coaching. That is the choice we have made. Teams, leadership and coaching rolling into one.

With the Mont Blanc circumnavigation under my belt it was time to ask one question. How far could I run in a day? Far had replaced fast as shorter distances lost their appeal. My first ultra marathon race was only three months away it was time to take my training to a new level. I had a couple of days free to run back to back marathons around the Gower Peninsula. With an overnight camp planned I set out with a pack weigh of 45lbs/20kgs. It was 08.30 in the morning and it was wet, very wet; my first two hours were slowed by my wetsuit like waterproofs. Come early morning the rain cleared and the weather would no longer put up a fight. 18 miles in and I reached my first option for an overnight camp, but I felt like my day had only just began. Although I had run out of water I enjoyed lunch and open beach running that would take me to the marathon mark (26.2 m/42k) and a water source. Perceptions weren't shifting they were being blown away.

Oblivious to many a holiday maker at Worms Head a well known spot, I was achieving something quite special. I was about to go further than the marathon distance, what's more I had done it drinking only two liters of water and carrying the equivalent of 20 bags of sugar. I had previously completed the marathon distance in a day and now I felt good to continue, I hooked in to my *iPod* and began marathon number two. The next ten miles was an undulating ride of coastal path running. Reaching the last opportunity for a decent camp spot I sat for a few minutes, but I was soon moving again. I am not sure if I really made any deals with myself but something inside me had set me on the trail of back to back marathons, just without any sleep.

At the 40 mile mark I was thwarted by a flooded river at the famous Three Cliffs Bay. In the dwindling light I now had to re-route, leaving the comfort of the coastal path for the tougher forest track. I knew this would mean I would be shy of back to back marathons but I figured 48 miles is not too shabby. Resigned to walking due to darkness and fatigue I returned home; ghost like at 11pm. The sausages that I had carried for the open fire would soon refuel me and then I pretended to sleep as my aching legs and wandering mind kept me awake until the small hours.

Prior to the 48 miles I was wondering when I would hit the infamous wall. Wondering, now there's a nice word that embodies the art of questioning. A quick search on the internet super highway gave me the following definition, "After running about 20 miles, wracked with total body fatigue, unsteadiness and possible light-headedness, a marathon runner hits an invisible wall, an apparently insurmountable physiological barrier which stops them in their tracks." Who could blame me for expecting to hit the wall? But, I didn't. Instead after about ten miles I noticed pain and fatigue; it was like reaching the top of a plateau. It was all about how long I was prepared to put up with the discomfort. With adequate physical fitness, a strong mental approach and self management during the event anything is possible. The wall? Rubbish, probably created by early marathon runners to exclude others. We agree 48 miles is of course an awful long way. However, much of that awful long way is due to the perceptions that we carry. As coachees we have the oppor-tunity to work with our perceptions. We have to explore unmarked territory, illustrate the lack of 'truth,' create new possibilities or set ourselves free from the current way of thinking.

Einstein talked of delusion and how we are trapped in our own prisons. Describing how we might free ourselves by 'widening our circle of compassion'. Surely the process and indeed purpose of coaching and asking questions is simply this? By committing to a physical action we immediately shift perception, thoughts and feelings.

Remember one of our earlier questions - how do you know there is a wall at 20 miles? This in itself is often enough to create a shift. Remember our conversations are highly sustainable. As *Rinpoche* observes when the 'jail keeper' is gone 'the jail would disappear and never be rebuilt again.' The wall? There is no wall. I know what I know having completed 48 miles of perception changing running. Don't believe the hype. Those that create the hype probably want to keep you locked up. Seek alternative possibilities, test these possibilities, personally. Enjoy creating this new landscape and boldly share it with others. They will appreciate your view. Be patient, these changes don't always happen at a flick of a switch. Be ready for surprises and celebrate them. Start before you are ready. Don't wait for your perception to be changed by someone else or from something you read. Get out there and run.

It's not about answers

What is beauty?
What is simple?
What is independence?
Where will you find acceptance?
How can you name this world?
What is your role?
What do you choose?
Who do you need to involve?
What game are you playing?
What feels natural?

What can you unlearn? What question is driving you?
How far can you go?
"Pride can stand a thousand trials
The Strong will never fall
But watching stars without you
My soul cries"
Kissing You - Des'ree

PART 5 – PERFORMANCE

Who are you being?

Performance

As your journey reaches its resting point performance will become the name of the game. Increasingly questions will dominate, who are you being? You will be observing and working constructively with three essential domains of human performance and existence - language, emotions and body. Knowingly or otherwise you have just stepped into the discipline of *ontology*. The study of being or existence.

You will already have experienced the first stage, *suspension*. In order to get back to your center, we have to stop spinning along the periphery. Suspend motion along our taken for granted ways of seeing the world. Then you can *redirect* your movements, a shift from outwards to inwards. The essence of performance change, perhaps being pulled by an imperceptible force within us, higher intentions. Destructive and creative processes at work. Bring into reality enduring performance *changes* that are both external and internal.

At the root of your *soul* you will find being. A place to rest during peak levels of performance. Relaxed and at ease with soul mates. Deep presence in your performance.

Clarity and freedom descend as your mind and body wanders. What once required conscious effort happens effort-lessly, almost automatically. Synchronizing the mind and *body*, performance now taking care of itself. Health and wealth combining. Vitality on the go. Wellbeing and being well.

Your *heart* is in it. Performance will not be achieved otherwise. Relationships, emotions, social interactions and confidence. The bonds we make, and those we break. Being intuitive, compassionate, trusting and empathetic.

A world view, planned and organized by the *mind*. Performance enhanced. Being study, research, reflection, learning, reading and writing. Logic pervades. Letters after your name, analyzed, assessed, certified sense.

A *spirit* that asks why are you being? A sometimes volatile extraction of our intentions. Performance shaped by beliefs, nature, creativity, actualization. Being sacred, sometimes scared. Diving deep, transformational.

Chapter 7

Goals

The gatekeeper

Having spent two years overseas my return to Swansea only lasted a week. I had to remain in transit otherwise I might get stuck. I chose a six-month stopover in London, my big trip had created a small town feel. The bright lights and the big city would capture me as my return ticket expired over ten years ago.

I got down to business, my coachability improved and more and more coaches would enter my world. Both of us being attracted to the challenge. Like me these coaches were armed with superior skills compared to what had gone before. This had to be the case, my demands were arguably greater and performance was stepping up.

One of my first managers used to coach me whilst he was driving, we had regional roles and all spent too much time on the road. If he didn't have to travel so much I wonder if he would ever have coached or talked to me at all. Towards the end of the conversations he would say 'oh, you've just made me think of...' Rubbish, he was just giving me his solutions, ones that rarely generated accountability. Where was Mr. Sanders' passion or Rob's equality? I left the organisation when my role was made redundant. He didn't even contact me, to this very day, nothing. Perhaps he didn't have much travel on at the time. He was not being authentic, he owned the coaching and the goals.

I had realized that both Mr. Sanders and Rob cracked the problem of the 'student teacher contradiction.' Rather than operating from these two poles we were both students and teachers, simultaneously. We were both accountable for the goals. Easy for me to do, after all I was the one trying to be more adult like. Not so easy for the unbiased referee or Scout Leader. We all know what happens when people are poles apart, but this is what happens when two people recognize and challenge the dichotomies. Inauthentic behaviors, political or otherwise were stifling the other coaches' efforts. Internally or externally driven, I do not know or care. All I know is that as coachee I was not getting what I needed and I lacked respect. I wanted to own the goals, partnership, joint ownership.

My new role gave me this exact opportunity. I was allowed to invest, it has been paying out ever since. As I shared my shares grew, the dividends never end. Performance related. Up until now I still had mostly been listening. Possibilities and perception explored in relative silence. Now I began opening up, talking, being vulnerable. It was hard to come by. I both loved and hated it. I was acutely aware that I was crossing a new threshold.

Enter Mo, an executive coach and facilitator. He had just won the contract to develop the internal coaching capability within the organization. He got me talking, firstly in groups as part of an authentic leadership program. I reveled in this new space, not bad because in the past I would have rebelled. Strange because I found it easier to open up with 10 people than I did one, less questions from the group of course. Mo had a meta question, 'who are you being?' It is a question I reflect on almost daily, confusing and searching. I guess therein lies this question's brilliance. Mo was unpredictable, a loose cannon that could go off at any time. He wasn't and isn't but that's how I initially responded to him. Like a buoy anchored to the ocean floor I bobbed above the surface and still refused to dive deep.

I soon realized Mo had unexplained power. He was immersed in the world of coaching. Declaring an ontological approach it appeared to me that he was the gatekeeper. Someone who could let me in, now and forever. That would be my goal. He had an aura about him that only now do I begin to understand. He would say something inspirational and then just leave it at that, problem solved, move on with confidence. He could see all angles (and probably angels), usually the ones that I did not think even existed. Metaphors skipped off his tongue like a poet and he was full of intrigue. He didn't seem to fit too well into everyday life, but the coaching sphere was his own.

I wanted a piece of this, but how could I get in? Would he let me in? As coachee I was showing bundles of enthusiasm, I would hang on his every word. Still listening. Then I learnt to talk, for real this time. With some skill and a dose of intent. We were in a coffee shop, just getting started on a coaching session. I was showing resistance, the kind of resistance that I had been showing for years. 'What's with all the questions?' I exclaimed. More thoughts of rebellion, mutiny even, echoes. Stop. This wasn't how I had planned on hoodwinking the gatekeeper, but here was my opportunity. 'What did you expect?' Mo's one liner calmly returned. That was it, I was hooked, I let rip and opened up. He had always told me to bring it on, I did, big style. He dealt with it, no big deal to him. To me I was breaking new ground, talking, verbalizing, crying. I was bringing it on, what would come up would come up. It would shake me to the core, liberated. I had started to consciously develop coachability.

This kind of moment and intent is at the core of our being. Entering somewhere new, liberated from the past. If life could be summarized in one word this would be it, freedom. From something, our emotions, thoughts and body. Of something, speech, choice, information. From the mad world where people run in circles. I could sense that *Narnia* like through the wardrobe exists a world where I would have the power to be, speak and think without hindrance or restraint. Enslaved no longer, liberty would beckon. An agent of choice, not control. I would determine my direction, a domino unwilling to fall. The gloves and chains were off. I had brought down the walls, no dark sarcasm in the classroom. I was going to be free, and I was going to have a good time. Drugs used to ease the pain, this time I wasn't going to get loaded. Now I would harness my freedom, it takes me higher and never lets me down.

Danger still lurked and the territory is still unknown but I had my protector. Maybe I would bump into a few monsters along the way, it would be OK.

'Mo, I kind of need you right now, I don't know how to deal with this. Yeah, well it's big smelly and troll like...' 'You know that guy Mo on the front gate, I'm with him...' 'I am not sure, let me speak to Mo...'

Mo had armed me with everything that I needed and I was off to the dungeon to see what I could find. After all I had been calling out from the dungeon for years. So maybe I had been talking after all, I just hadn't found the right person to talk to. That was it, in Mo I had someone I knew who could hold me to account. He was dealing with plenty of things himself, like his health, but I could talk to him. Even my riddles made sense to him. Fireworks were going off in my head and a new arena beckoned...

Dot, dot, dot... I didn't know how this was going to end, even my sentences had opened up. Mo was getting me to express and challenge my reality and perception. Head scratching questions, grounding me in the present and battling the illusory past and future states. In hindsight I was also beginning my journey from coachee to coach. My riddles subsided and I began to articulate. The art of speaking, fluent in English, coherent in my story. Connecting, expressing and pronouncing.

Mo likened my role to that of *Neo* played by *Keanu Reeves* in the film *The Matrix*. Did Mo know that I was a fan of this film? Probably not, he didn't need to know, he just knew. It's the question that drives us; yup you can tell I am driven by his questions. The answer is up there; well it is now that I have the ability to open up and talk. It will find you if you want it to; absolutely I would never have allowed 'it' in previously. The time has come to make a choice.

Like *Neo* I was impatient, wondering where this journey would take me next. "Why do my eyes hurt? You've never used them before. Rest *Neo* the answers are coming." More important than what is when. If Mo had a meta question he also had a micro question, typically towards the end of our conversations. 'By when?'

Mo would work with my reality. 'What is real?' 'How do you define real?' 'It's hell at work at the moment,' I would declare.

'What, really. It's a place of suffering and punishment in the afterlife?' Confidently waiting for my response.

'No, of course not. You know what I mean.' Silence, point made. Reality and metaphors need to be assessed in more detail.

"What are you waiting for? Stop trying to hit me and hit me." I did numerous times, bring it on. Of course my ability to talk wasn't always a skillful one. Mo was my protector. I trusted him, I could count on him. "You have to trust me... you know that road, you know exactly where it ends and I know that's not where you want to be. I imagine right now you are feeling a bit like *Alice*." Not Mo's words exactly but he had given me the choice between two pills - red to learn the truth, blue to return to the world as I know it. Like *Neo* I had accepted by swallowing the red pill. Performance-enhancing. Although I did not subsequently find myself in a liquid filled pod, my body connected by wires and tubes to a vast mechanical tower covered with identical pods. I wasn't in *The Matrix* but Mo's world did depict a future in which reality as perceived by most humans is actually a simulated reality.

Building on the platform of authenticity Mo encouraged me to be honest and to see the world of coaching for myself. He couldn't tell me what this world was like. I had to walk through it, he was merely showing me the door. It started with a glimpse inside, then a few short walks, not wandering too far from the portal. Finally being comfortable to be. Not thinking, knowing. I let it all go, fear, doubt and disbelief. I was freeing my mind and thinking like a beginner. Unlearning everything I had learnt in order to adapt to this new environment. How could I sustain contradictions? I would have to they are endless.

'But what are the results?' Not a typical Mo question, too pragmatic, one of mine actually. In *The Matrix*, Neo asks, "What are you trying to tell me, that I can dodge bullets?" His mentor *Morpheus* replies "No *Neo* I'm trying to tell you that when you're ready you won't have to." The same was true for me. Half the time I didn't have a clue to the relevance of our conversations. I couldn't see the goal. When the time came I did. I was prepared before the fall.

Like *Neo* my time in this new reality was starting to change, open up and grow. I was experiencing the early signs of a duality. I was clearly a coachee with Mo and clearly a coach in my role at work. If I wasn't taking anyone else on my journey then I was missing the point entirely. It is no use gaining enlightenment and taking a vow of silence. The closing shot of the film, a telephone box just like the one where my journey began. *Neo* answers the call, "I know you are out there, I can feel you now, I know that you are afraid, you're afraid of us, you're afraid of change. I don't know the future, I didn't come here to tell you how this is going to end, I came here to tell you how this is going to begin. I'm going to hang up this phone and then I'm going to show these people what you don't want them to see. I'm going to show them a world without you, a world without rules and controls without borders or boundaries. A world where anything is possible. Where we go from there is a choice I leave to you.

Ah the synchronicities of another telephone box, not Devon and bad news this time. No, instead Sydney, Australia where I was living and where *The Matrix* was being filmed. I used to walk past that phone box everyday on my way to and from work. It was next to my bank, commuters, bustle, elaborate underground train stations. Synchronicity, something that as coachee and coach I was soon to get used to.

Performance goals

'You are either accountable or you aren't,' my manager once told me. I found it quite strange that a Learning professional would dismiss the possibility that it is a learnable value. The first program I worked on that had any kind of depth to it was an accountability program developed in the US. We worked with individual and team accountability, it spread like wildfire through the organisation to the point that demand was outstripping our ability to supply. When you are a coachee accountability really boils down to your goals.

In the West we work with a goals first, energy second approach. The Eastern approach prioritizes energy first goals second. Or, even better energy and goals simultaneously. There are plenty of people who have lots of goals, they think that is enough, but if they don't have energy they rarely get achieved. On the flip side people have an abundance of energy but lack the rigor of goals to channel their intent. A fairly common pattern is that in our teenage years we have bundles of energy but no goals. Often as the goals surface the energy diminishes. Maybe the reality of a goal scares us and ensures that the energy leaks out elsewhere.

In the West of course we focus perhaps more on goal achievement than our energy. Questions like, 'how is the project going?' seem to direct us towards a time and space answer. Unlikely to generate a response that opens up our emotions and motivation. 'How is pre season training going?' elicit responses that ignore our hunger, confidence or excitement for the fixtures ahead. How many times have you asked someone 'what are you doing?' plenty I am sure. How many times have you inquired, 'who are you being?' As a coachee I now look to secure my goals towards the ends of conversation, rather than at the start. If the goal is misjudged then you are miss-aligned. Again hold the question, be curious, open and the goal will emerge. Goals without energy or energy without goals, neither works well.

A well known story of goals and energy is portrayed in the film *Karate Kid*. *Daniel LaRusso* moves with his mother to Los Angeles. Their apartment's handyman is an odd but kindly and humble Okinawan immigrant, *Mr. Miyagi*. When *Miyagi* witnesses *Daniel* getting beaten up by school bullies, he intervenes. In awe *Daniel* asks *Miyagi* to be his coach, his goal to learn Karate. *Miyagi* doesn't attend to his goal initially, instead his energy. Asking *Daniel* to perform monotonous chores such as the famous 'wax on, wax off' scene, sanding a wooden floor, refinishing a fence and painting his house. Each task is accompanied with a specific movement, such as clockwise/counter-clockwise hand motions. *Miyagi* is developing *Daniel's* energy, unknown to our departing coachee who is desperate to 'work on his goal.' When he expresses his frustration, *Miyagi* reveals that *Daniel* has been learning defensive blocks through muscle memory learned by performing the chores. The rest is Hollywood history.

'What's that budget line for?' I inquire.

'That's the funds for the Director's mentor.' A short, matter of fact response.

'What's their relationship like?' I probe further, sensing concealment.

'I think they have contact each month face to face or over the phone. The mentor has worked in retail in a previous role and is mentoring some of the other Directors. I think this is their ninth year of working together.'

This was a casual conversation with one of my managers, I was advising them on how to consolidate their training budget. Nine years sounds like dependency and addiction to me, whereas I want to see goals being achieved. Without getting too far ahead of themselves a coachee has to plan for the next steps. To witness an improvement in performance and make the transition from working with a coach to being independent. That's not to say you cannot pick up with the same or a different coach in the future. Planning your 'goodbyes' may be as important as your 'hellos'.

I remember getting caught out myself. After I graduated, I met Alan who was South African. He was a great friend and I admired his approach to life. Not many backpackers make it as far as Wales, he did and he stayed. He fueled my desire to travel and my interest in South Africa. I bumped into one of the guys I had played hockey with at University and he asked me when I was going overseas. My heart sunk, I realized that if my hockey mates knew about my plans I must have been telling a lot of people. Alas, there was not any real substance behind them. Goals yes, energy no. As *Yoda* our little green friends from *Star Wars* said, "Do, or do not. There is no try." I was not going anywhere near the African continent, I was trying and I hadn't been accountable for my talk. It wasn't until our honeymoon that I would take Alan's advice and explore the Cape. My round the world trip was always well fueled. However, apart from a SE Asia guidebook I had no clear intent. Andy presented me with the opportunity to develop this goal and I remember clearly writing down one, three, and five year plans. At the time I likened them to the five year plans for the National Economy of the Soviet Union. Like *Khrushchev* I needed a bit of a dictator to carry out my reform. A memorable drafting of a pros and cons list opened up new land.

If you are trying you aren't succeeding. Place an object on a surface in front of you, such as a pen on a desk. Now pick up the object. Great, put it back down. Now pick up the object. Fantastic, you are getting the hang of this, again return it to its spot. Pick up the object, more success. Now start over with the object on the surface again. Now try and pick up the object. Your default is to probably pick it up. Unfortunately, that is not *trying* to pick up the object that is picking up the object as you have done before. Trying to pick up the object never involves actually picking it up as you did three times successfully beforehand.

One of the finest exhibitions of developing coachability that I was privileged enough to be a part of was with Sarah and Steve. They were planning to climb Everest in aid of UNICEF, goals don't come much bigger. As a keen, if somewhat amateur mountaineer I have always been fascinated by Everest and how I might contribute to a successful expedition. I began researching planned expeditions for the following year to offer my services for free. Within days I was in touch with Sarah to agree the way forward. Being coached had actually been part of their original plan but it had been scrapped due to a lack of budget.

Steve in particular personified accountability. He was making the rapid shift from coachee to coach. Rapid by his standards given that when we first started talking he was not particularly au fait with the coaching world. Yet he had the raw talent in abundance. In turn he proved to me that he was definitely coachable. A value that would certainly serve him on his expedition. He would expect only the best coaching from me, this drove my practice skywards. He would gently analyze the content of our conversations, yet remain open to the application. Towards the end of our last three sessions I asked Steve to participate in quantum exercises. Ones that would embed the learning by applying the natural laws of energy. I slowly picked up that he was using these very same exercises in the seven days between our conversations with a colleague at work.

The dangerous conditions in the Khumbu Icefall and on the Lhotse Face forced the team to abandon its expeditions to Everest, Lhotse and Nuptse for the entire season. However, Sarah and Steve had received somber news a few months beforehand when they failed to raise enough funds for the trip. As coachees they remain accountable. Bringing a smile to my face they have a new goal and new energy - to become qualified coaches. They are at the foot of another mountain.

This lasting thought gives us a great insight in how to articulate goals - as metaphors or analogies. Accessible and resonant. Metaphors are great for explanation or clarification, often connecting on an unconscious level. A figure of speech in which a word or phrase is applied to an object or action to which it is not literally applicable. 'I had fallen through a trapdoor of depression.' Likewise analogies that make a comparison between two similar things, such as coaching and mountains. I encourage coachees to work with analogies and metaphors, as they can be incredibly powerful. Search for them and ask for them.

I remember an author who described her approach to work. She was a 'non scientist' interviewing quantum physicists. They would use words to describe the situation. She would grasp some of the concepts but to check her understanding or further her grip she would ask for or provide an analogy or metaphor. If you accept someone else's or develop your own then accountability and performance can increase ten fold. Remember these can limit your also, just as I described to Mo how work was 'hell like.'

Paying attention to how words are constructed can in turn help you construct your goals. Responsibility, accountability and empowerment for example. Responsibility is one step away from accountability. The meaning of the word suggests having a duty or having control over someone. The key word buried in the main word is a word we have already looked at - response. Here we expect someone to respond with action. RESPONSE-ability. Of course the key word in accountability, is count. I can count on you to fulfill a task without the need for me to provide direction in which you must respond. A clear sign that coachability has been achieved. aCOUNTability. Beyond this there is another level, empowerment. No need to point out the hidden text this time. The coachee has assumed power and will take care of his or her actions. EmPOWERment.

To build this into an example picture a familiar scene in a restaurant where a customer complains. The staff that have to ask their manager how to respond are of course responsible. Those that take care of the situation are accountable, although they will still update the manager on when they have been counted on.

Those with power again deal with the customer's needs, this time their manager rarely needs to be informed.

It was the question that Rob the Scout leader asked, 'what do you think?' that shifted a responsibility conversation to an accountable one. The coachee could now progress in a different way. Likewise you can progress in a different way. This chapter might have ended but really it's only starting, as soon as you crack performance goals it is probably time to set mastery goals.

Signing up for a 100 kilometers (62 miles) event was always going to be a landmark in my running career, my boldest goal to date. Considerably longer than any one-day event that I previously attempted, the route would also include 2,000 meters of ascent across the South Downs in England. As a team of four we were also committed to raising £2,000 worth of sponsorship for the *Gurkha Welfare Trust*.

After only five hours sleep most of the campsite seemed to be awake by 4am. I for one could have stayed tucked up in my sleeping bag until 5.55am giving me five minutes to hit the start line. It wasn't to be, wiping the sleep from my eyes we set out. No need for a warm up or breakfast, both can take care of themselves later on.

When things go wrong, they go wrong and the ensuing drama unfolds. For me this event went as smoothly as it could do despite its length. My goals were aligned to my energy. Maybe it comes down to luck and/or an attention to detail but I seemed to escape the ordeals that the rest of my team experienced. About half way round, the miles began to take their toll. Dai was stricken with cramp. For the first time in my life I observed someone going from an upright running position to lying on the floor as both hamstrings spasmed. I gave Dai some electrolyte tablets that I had been taking with my water from the start of the race and they seemed to do the trick. Putting his Chamonix hospital adventures behind him Chris was suffering in the heat and beginning to cramp also. A conscious intake of water and switch to a technical t-shirt kept him on the trail. Our final team member Lee floated around the first 50 miles but started getting his own dose of cramps, stomach cramps. On inquiry we would realize that he had only eaten a pack of sweets all day. As a team we could offer no real help but to allow him 20 minutes in a portaloo whilst we enjoyed a cup of tea. With five miles to go I jogged down a small hill, wincing in pain, forward motion mixed with the sideways movement of wanting to stop. Something felt wrong, really wrong, completely different to the last 57 miles or so. I stopped, nearing a panic. No one was with me. Instead 200 meters behind me my compatriots were limping down the same hill, looking like vagrants tanked up on cider. If I had the energy to laugh I would have.

Challenging goals are part and parcel of endurance events and they didn't prevent us from exceeding expectations. We came 14th out of 450 teams in a time of 13 hours 46 minutes. A Gurkha team won in 10 hours and 30 minutes, and military outfits occupied the top 12 places. The team in front of us were semi professional athletes who lived in the French Alps. Even though I was used to finishing in the top 10 – 20 per cent of events this was easily my best and most satisfying placing to date. I was curious as to why I felt so good. I could pinpoint one area; overwhelmingly my goals for the event were authentic. By this I mean my internal values were matched by just about everything that I experienced. The weather, South Downs scenery and team morale met my needs perfectly. One thing really stood out for me; the Gurkha connection. With my love for Nepal raising money for this courageous culture was amazing and to spend time with them on the run and at the checkpoints was special. Their smile, graceful running styles and support did not go unnoticed.

Given that all participants were raising money for the same cause it created a solidarity like I have never seen before. Competing teams talked, laughed and shared. At one point three teams were in hot pursuit when we reached a navigation decision. We paused, from 400 meters behind I could see someone pointing to the right. They showed us the way when they could easily have overtaken. Being attuned to the event's meaning in this way gave it greater depth and it allowed me to be free in different ways; self management, leadership and consciousness. Self-management is often understated. Maintaining your vitality during peak periods or projects barely gets a look in. Ignore this at your peril, during an ultra marathon even the smallest blind spot can be the difference between success and failure. Electrolytes, technical T-shirts and energy bars could have prevented some of the team challenges. It takes planning and the constant act of self-monitoring to achieve, but crucially you are the best placed person to do this.

When you are in a state of flow leadership comes naturally. It manifests itself as a state of being, not doing. Nicely described by *Lin Yutang*, "Being over doing, character over achievement, and calm over action." Being is fundamental to our existence and world orientation. *Erich Fromm* a renowned psychologist explains that being is to do with our character, our total orientation to life; it is a state of inner activity. "One of aliveness and authentic relatedness." We didn't have a team hierarchy as such, probably because we had always looked to Gary for the traditional leadership role. He was the most experienced member of our team but he had to pull out a few weeks prior with an injury. Time for me to step up to the plate. I managed our pace, organized check point activity and navigated the route. Subtle differences that allowed the rest of the team to focus on their needs. I was being a leader, goals in check.

It is rarely written or spoken about, but during endurance events many athletes will take ibuprofen tablets to manage the pain and reduce swelling. Towards the end of the race Chris asked me for two tables. I shared them willingly but told him to recognize when they start to relieve the pain. Otherwise, why bother? Celebrate their effects. In other words consciousness.

You have to pay a lot of attention to consciousness, but in our busy lives we often remain ignorant. With its links to self management, we assume consciousness requires no attention. Conversely consciousness is what gives attention.

David Bohm the theoretical physicist assumes consciousness itself "Requires very alert attention or else it will simply destroy itself. It's a very delicate mechanism." Tune in and be mindful of your feelings and surroundings, attention will be simultaneous. In order to develop authentic goals, consider the compatibility between you and your environment. Extract the word city from authenticity and you can see why creating an authentic community is so important. Build this network from solid foundations, solidarity.

It's not about trying

What do you expect?

By when?

What are you waiting for?

What are you goals?

Where is your energy?

How can you say goodbye?

How can you stop trying?

Who will respond?

Who can you count on?

Where does the power lie?

Can you describe it as a metaphor?

What do you think?

Where does authenticity lie?

Where can you find solidarity?

Chapter 8

Systems

Return of the king

I emerged from *The Matrix* after what seemed like an inordinate amount of time. You know when you go somewhere new, time seems to stand still. You are in awe of its beauty not wanting to leave. It took me a while to take stock of what I had discovered. Mo was highly intuitive, I loved that. It was my preference also, just less developed. I had to take these great ideas and ground them in the real world.

The opportunity arose as part of my Masters in Human Resources and Development. I chose to research the role of the internal coach for my dissertation, based on where I was working at the time. I knew I wouldn't be able to use Sci-Fi quotes in this context so I set out to read all that I could on coaching. This was a wonderful opportunity to scour every well referenced book or article on coaching at the time. Given that the literature and research in this growing industry was relatively small, I was able to absorb these 50 plus resources pretty quickly 'how do you know what you know (about coaching)?' Well there you have it Mo, easily quantifiable.

As well as the literature I interviewed coaches and coachees within the organisation. I reduced coaching to its simplest level; listening, questioning, feedback and observation. Now I had some clarity. I also delivered the bad news that a coaching culture had not (yet) been achieved within the organisation. It was clear to me that organizations need to take an intuitive and logical approach to developing internal coaches. To achieve this I started drawing a map to represent this area of coaching. A collection of data showing the spatial arrangements and distribution of habitats and habits. It can represent a sequence of events if you like. Its purpose like many maps is to help us navigate the new. Taking us from one culture to another, new dimensions. Going beyond mental maps so that we can share the journey with others. Transformational. Deep structures, developing as surface structures, so that they can be seen and accessed more easily. The sub processes of language, language maps. Describing the journey from knowing coaching, to doing to being. Tailored for different explorers be they individual, teams or organisations.

My dissertation would soon be in the bag, I had 6 months left to write it up. Of course my undergraduate studies had also been beautifully on course. Then they weren't. So why should my postgraduate studies be any different. Another journey would begin, my role was being made redundant. Again. I was 32 years old and two of my roles had been sidelined. I would soon be walking down a different street.

Regardless, my dissertation and I marched on. It was one aspect of the research that kept me awake. Like so many research projects it was one thing that I had unearthed, unexpected and surprised. I asked all of the coachees that I interviewed the same question. 'how have you benefited as a result of the coaching?' The usual responses were clocking up, leadership, confidence, relationships etc. There was one surprise, which came up every time. 'I have developed as a coach.' Unsolicited.

Coachees developing as coaches, a new system was emerging. My 20,000 word dissertation had come down to these four words. It was here that I began to connect the two. We must develop coachees to be become better coaches. Just as much as we must develop coaches to become better coachees. The two are the same, there's just an extra letter E separating these words. Now I had something, that is what I call research. Of course I still needed a Talent Programme and rugby coaching to turn my thoughts into words.

Struggling to write a dissertation about an organisation that I no longer worked for actually presented me with yet another opportunity. I was presenting my findings at the *Chartered Institute of Personnel and Development* annual *Coaching at Work Conference*. This would be my very last act as a full time employee, one that they would not even know or care about. I finished my presentation, took a deep breath and began to contemplate my new future. The future tapped me on the shoulder at lunch. 'Hi, I am Martin, I work for one of the largest charities in the UK. I was really interested in your presentation...' Another new system to explore. Dot, dot dot...

Looking back maybe I did give myself a hard time for not talking more. Because in reality I reckon I was doing quite a good job as coachee. I hadn't fallen down the hole, I had come out the other side of losing my Mum a much stronger individual. I now know that I was considering possibilities, challenging perception and changing performance. Considering is what I was doing, the vehicle to get me there. Possibilities were my world, my point in time and space. Awareness was who I was being, enough said. So I was doing something in space and time to be someone. Doing, space and time, being.

I had crossed another line but there was no ceremony to notice. I needn't have feared, Mo had prepared me for this moment, or at least he was beginning to prepare me. A few weeks previously I had sent out an email to all my suppliers to let them know about my change in circumstances. My deeper intention was to put the feelers out for possible jobs. Within minutes from sending the email one of my suppliers had called offering me some work that would tap into my outdoor and leadership skills. My network had delivered.

The word consultancy sent a shiver down my spine. Like many things in life that which terrifies us draws us in. A new system that I wanted to be a part of. I soon realized where my performance could take me. Day one I was enjoying three new challenges. My first day as a consultant, my first piece of work in

Scotland and my first assignment within local government. If I had planned to develop all three systems on one day I surely would have resisted the challenge. Mo's support had enabled me to not only smash the performance barriers but to also excel. Six months later the client confessed, 'the only reason we keep using you is because you understand local government so well.' I had a hard time keeping the smile off my face, one of joy and one of surprise. I did not present my confession about the newness of it all, this did not seem to matter.

One perception did however, limit my beliefs. My first test in this new role was self constructed; I believed I was too young to go solo. Without disclosing this to Mo he gave me some feedback. 'you are good on your feet, you live in London and you're young.' Whoa, wait a minute that is precisely my problem, I lack grey hair. Within minutes my perception had shifted, my youth represented my unique selling point and I had better hurry up and get out there as I am growing older by the minute. I had held the C word as a possibility and now my performance started to change. Test completed, the self-constructed barrier had now transformed itself in to a launch pad. Weeks turned into months, months into years, three years to be precise. Continual performance.

Mo was there to support me, and I was there to support Mo, symbiosis personified. But, his timing was impeccable. As *Joseph Campbell* writes in *The Hero with a Thousand Faces* "The hero is covertly aided by the advice, amulets, and secret agents of the supernatural helper whom he met before his entrance into this region." He was busy building my profile and leading lines of inquiry that would raise my performance. Mo would stand by me as I would stand by him. It was one thing that he would commend my services, it was another for me to follow.

I absolutely flourished in my first Scottish winter enjoying great success with the project. I was still looking for permanent roles which also kept me busy. In May I went back to Nepal, more straightforward this time but no less significant on where it would take me. In my time there I discovered the ultimate prize, my possibilities had not only shifted, they had changed. It did so with ease, suggesting that Mo had primed me for superior choices. Where others might have faced a test my elect encounters of the last few months ensured I had made no mistake.

There was no enlightenment moment sitting in the Khumbu Valley looking out across Everest. Although that was good and is worthy of such a defining label. Instead with the Scottish project laying fallow for a few months and the job search going cold, in the Himalayas I had realized something. Mo had realized it long ago. After eight months of job hunting I hadn't found my perfect role. Why? It didn't exist. Well, not in a permanent way, I was fulfilling my perfect role. The life of a consultant. Freelance and autonomous.

As I would notice in the years to come my possibilities and perception would flip. Beforehand, permanent work would have been my first priority, freelance work second. Now freelance work sat at the top of the tree and the permanent possibilities would soon fall from the tree like rotting fruit. Sounds harsh but conversing with recruitment agencies and showing up for job interviews lacking any drive was akin to accidentally biting into a rotten apple that tasted like battery acid. I had difficultly removing some of this rotten flesh. Trying to shake off an agency that had lined me up for an interview was like trying to move on from a dose of Nepalese food poisoning. When possibilities are out of alignment in a relationship it can be tough. They were desperate to fill their interviewee quotient for the role and I was keen to advance my consultancy dream. Had I come so far? Now a dream, when only eight months ago it would have been a nightmare.

I was taking a stand for my values. When I was five years old I used to go and sit in my Dad's car, a BMW. I would play around with the paper receipts that inhabited this ecosystem, pretending to work. The car on one hand was a mess with work stuff, on the other it provided me with the tools for my early employment. This memory says a lot about my values, I valued autonomy amongst other things. Mo would ask 'when did you first identify a value?' My unpaid job would serve to this effect. The next question was the killer one, 'when did you first take a stand for this value?' Action, the difference between recognizing and living. An opportunity to appreciate why we are who we are. Why we need to be who we need to be. Why after 3 years into my consultancy business I had to buy a BMW that would often see me working in the passenger seat with my laptop. Parked at the side of a road, in car parks and service stations. A young boy in adults clothing. A new and familiar ecosystem that reaches our very core. Consciously or unconsciously fueling our intent.

On my return from Nepal it was time to deal with another performance question that had found its way into my network. I needed to speak to Martin from the conference. I had been resisting this for some time as the potential prize could set me up for a while. An ongoing consultancy role, almost part time in nature. A role that could be the stepping stone from no work to secure work and ad hoc consultancy. Mo had been instrumental in helping me to create this vision. It could be the perfect situation. I would have money coming in three days a week and the flexibility to set up my business and commit to other work. On one side of the bank lay my present situation and on the other consultancy. A bold move to make, even with my triathlon training I didn't fancy this open water swim. Instead I would start to build a bridge, spanning my perception gap. Like a video game the bridge would soon crumble from behind, blocking my return and pushing me forwards. I would still get wet. The cold water wouldn't shock me or leave me short of breath. Still a gap, still possibilities.

Systems emerge and bring us a step forward. If I could have

chosen a way to enter the freelance system this would have been it. I had to bring this back, I had to secure the role, it could nourish everything else that I wanted to do. Being an environmental charity I could not have been more authentic if I had tried.

I spent the morning swimming in the London's Serpentine, Hyde Park, training for a summer of triathlons. As well as the new physical challenges I enjoyed the social aspect to the sport, in some way replacing what I had left behind with my work colleagues. Our swim training was famous for a social interaction I had never anticipated. People have been swimming in the Serpentine for hundreds of years, photos of the Christmas morning swim with snow on the ground in the early 1900s are a testament to their resolve. One thing they won't tell you about is the mixed changing facilities. A five meter square changing room hosts the daily mix. During my debut I noticed a lady in the changing room, then I noticed her next action. I thought to myself this looks fun. Then I realized it was my turn and my chuckle melted into a coy change.

One morning after a now polished mini triathlon of change/swim/change my training partner Enzo and I set out on a short cycle ending up at his apartment for breakfast. Enzo was also self employed, of course being open to possibilities I fed off his observations as well as feeding off his kitchen table. We had eaten melon, apparently professional tri-athletes do the same. I felt in a really good space, melon eating amateur tri-athlete and business entrepreneur. Then Martin called. I walked onto the balcony finding space as I always do on the phone, looking out across the Notting Hill views and shared apartment gardens. It was negotiating time, Martin was a skilled negotiator but authenticity reigned once again. I told him a part or full time role would not suit me as I needed flexibility.

Also the salary needed to be higher. I had put the brakes on the one thing I so desperately needed. I was not really negotiating as I did not have any alternatives or the option to barter for another outcome. Maybe I had eaten too much melon, or maybe Mo had gotten to the core of what I needed as well as the obvious wants. Martin said maybe there is another way, this unlocked everything. I had penetration and traction, reaching the source of my needs.

I went back to Mo that evening telling him that I had a problem. Unashamedly ripping him off I described that there are two problems being a consultant. The first problem is not having enough work, the second is having too much. We celebrated being in the latter camp. That was the moment I probably started to graduate from Mo's class. At the time of writing our contact remains intermittent. Perhaps I had conquered enough performance challenges under his guidance for now. Although I have a strange feeling that our time will come again.

I had just finished delivering a workshop in Edinburgh and I was making my way to my hotel for the evening. John my new job share called. A call of no great significance other than the recognition that I was competently running two large consultancy projects simultaneously, two systems not one. I got back to my hotel and completed an evening's work based on John's recommendations. It was like both clients had given me their blessing, knowing about my commitments to each project. It was sometimes comical where and how I worked so that both were fulfilled. In the car park in the hours proceeding a triathlon; energy drink in one hand mobile in the other hamstring being stretched looking at my bike. The energy drink had given me a sign. I had been reading about sports nutrition. One of its mantras was replacement versus replenishment, "we cannot replace everything we expend during exercise, but we can keep ourselves going all day long if we replenish appropriately." I was replacing energy, yet with the demands of two systems I was unable to fully replenish.

Metaphorically speaking Mo had to come and get me, he

found me slumped by the side of the road. I had 'bonked out' and run my energy reserves dry. I was immersed in both projects yet hadn't kept an eye on the future. I had cast off the reality of setting up a business, why would I want to return? I favored the bliss like state of abundant work with familiar clients. I had found paradise but hadn't planned my next trip. 'What happens when one or both of these projects finish?' he would ask. I would listen, but it took a while before my performance changed on this one. He summoned me almost, I delayed, sealed in by my perfect state. I didn't need to leave this entirely, just dip out once in a while get my head above the water and then go back under for a few more strokes.

Soon my response would shift 'there will always be another project to replace it,' I would reply. A sound factual statement, but what was lacking was the active energy in finding this new project. So with Mo's guidance my business development activities began and still bear fruit today. Mo helped me to create my business vision. Lean, flexible and valued. Ignoring for now chasing the transition from small to medium to large scale. Mo's words ringing in my ears 'when you are somewhere in the middle it's hard to make a decent living.'

To honor this commitment to action I placed one of my favorite systems in my consciousness for good. I quickly called my business *Storm Beach*. Like the beach the organisation would be based on authenticity, energy and change. Just a name but one that would resonate with me like no other. Two words that would ensure I was tied to the beach for good and all that it represents. I was unsure whether it would work in the business world, but I had started and I would learn by my mistakes if I had to.

Performance systems

Having left the light polluted London skies I was admiring the cosmos whilst camping in South West England. The star spotted sky reminded me of personal and work systems. The network is king, I would tell myself. NetworKING. As I retreated further into my duck down sleeping bag it occurred to me that I had all the resources I needed in my systems, they didn't exist in some far off galaxy. Like the sky above I could see and access them all. For the time being it was a case of working with my network rather than expanding it. Yet by definition it's like the cosmos, constantly expanding, I was just focusing on whom I knew. Snuggled in my bag I had no desire to formally inspect the word cosmos, but I do remembering it referring to a system with order and harmony. Perfect just what I was after. On the train home my desire to inspect the word was matched by my Wi-Fi capabilities. Another synchronicity appeared, in Mandarin Chinese, cosmos is translated as yuzhou. Literally translated this means space-time.

As the months and years clocked by many a contact would emerge from my network. Some surprising, some intended. The dormant phase could easily be explained by the global recession. Lots of good contacts nourished waiting for the right environment to flourish. It could be less quantifiably observed as a result of the intentions that I had engineered. Either way it required patience and a focus on the present moment. The long term view struggling for supremacy over the short. Confidence in the cosmos, traveling at the speed of sound. Unknowing in the universe, traveling at the speed of light. I am certainly a hitch-hiker, with only a rough guide to the galaxy. A lonely planet, but linked to the whole.

As a coachee's performance shifts so does their system. Increasingly in size and complexity. A great performance indicator. Compounded of several parts, members and others systems, one can morph with ease. Interacting, interdependent, integrated, all showing off your coachability. Defined by structure, sometimes rigid, sometimes loose. Behaviors that are whole, not hole. Total, union, crowd. Like a body of water allow elements in and let elements out. Risk pollution, with fluidity and exit systems you can mitigate. Recognize that you are experiencing emotions nothing more, do not let the pollutants take hold. Risking stagnation, a gamble not worth betting on. Some systems readily nourish. Encourage new surroundings, symbiosis. Some threaten. Notice their boundaries, parasites. Some might influence you, some you will shift. Collaboration required on both counts, openness, confidence even.

Developing coachability has to have some impact on the immediate system, easily recognised as one's network. As your performance develops who has noticed or benefitted also? Are you growing your network as you seek out like minded and different people. If you are looking for a return on investment then this is the space in which to find it. Add some time intentions and there we have it, evaluation. Just like my star gazing evening you have to observe the change in performance. You might need the *Hubble* telescope to do this or a quick glance in the right direction will suffice. As an amateur astronomer it's OK to sit in your conservatory with your kaleidoscope!? Ill equipped at first.

Now for the subtlety, which system are you progressing? The existing one or a new one. This comes back to a space question, where are you investing your energy and is it in the right place. Consider for example, an organization's strategy or vision that is written, developed and worked towards. Are you impacting on this system? If so you will notice the strategy and organization grow to a point of maturity, however, from there on it will decline. Unless of course another strategy develops. This happens alongside the current initiative as individuals are the first to research and develop a new area of knowledge or activity. Like the pioneers of the Wild West they open up and begin to settle in new terrain, colonists, explorers and trailblazers. The original system goes into decline and the urge amongst its protagonists is to protect. Pioneers from the new system start to connect with each other until they gain enough momentum to progress.

Somewhere along the line you will find the tipping point. What we really need here is protection from the original system not for itself but for the new system as there is often a gap between the rise and fall of the two systems. It is during this gap that people can get hurt until the new system is set in motion ready to break new ground. Your energy doesn't have to be in this new system but it is worth knowing where your energy is, two systems thinking. If you lose your house keys walking home one night, don't just spend your time searching under lamp posts where the light is good. Your search is likely to be in the wrong place, the lights this time might not guide you home.

You can access any network you want. Who are all these people speaking at conferences, publishing articles and appearing on TV? They are just like me, just like you, although their networks are probably creating these opportunities. If you want to enter this circle all you have to do is ask. Look at your network, there might be people who are not red hot on your radar but can connect you. You are only once removed. Make contacts and set up the connection. All the recipient can say is, yes, no or maybe.

The more you work with a coach the larger and richer your system can become. Your intentions towards your network can also fundamentally differ, actively connecting people rather than being the one set up. Social networking offers boundary less communication and sharing of intentions. From an evaluation point of view you will know that the coaching is having a profound effect on your performance when your systems change.

When you connect others you may start to wonder 'what do I get in return?' Patience and trust is required, likewise this is what you get in return. Maybe they will continue conversations without you. However, they will always be linked to your system, maybe eclipsing your opportunities. When will they repay you with a connection of your own? An ego that fights for survival but needs to be kept under control. You might not need to be precise as to how the recommendation will be repaid, you don't need that. You can find a way to qualify it and that is enough. A return on investment of 5 per cent does not apply here. Demand that your system serves others. In turn you will be served, nourished and enriched. A noticeable shift is required, growing up one tends to only be aware on how you are being served. Food, water, shelter and warmth. Positions of education serving you, positions in work serving you. The noticeable shift of when you first serve a family member, hidden in a supportive way, obvious in a challenging way. Ask yourself, 'how can you serve your coach?' and in turn the benefits are mutual.

Other systems may not offer obvious connections. If it's a person you might not actually like them, or need to like them. For example, I have seen lots of coachees drawn to work with coaches due to the value that they could add. How they could enrich their system. An odd position, they would not always look forward to seeing them yet they knew they could benefit. Certain aspects of their approach they might connect with, certain aspects may leave them asking questions. I suppose this sums up the support and challenge model. One minute you will be hanging on their every word as coachee yet wish they would be more professional in their planning and communication. Baffled at their odd dress sense or business intent. Personal, picky and maybe pointless holding these perceptions. As long as it is not enough to stop you from working together. Perhaps this point of difference offers the space for coaching.

As well as noticing the performance benefits, it is also important to be mindful of how your system can serve another. We are servants first, this is fundamental to any relationship. Coachee serving coach and coach serving coachee. When you begin any coaching relationship ask yourself 'what will the coach learn from you?' If you were to share this with your coach, it can often catch them by surprise, it is not meant to. They expect their role will serve yours, naturally the construct for coaching. Yet they must be served also, we are back to *Freire's* views on dialogue and joint exploration. We all need to make sure that other people's highest priority needs are being met. The emergent agenda is shared, we are both growing, developing and changing. Energy in and energy out. Community and fellowship that carefully grooms needs, ensuring one side is not more heavily weighted than the other. To achieve this listening must come first, performance challenged and hierarchy shelved. Embodying the Roman tradition where the leader is, "First among equals."

In order to really transform your performance maybe you will need to engage with some systems that are new, different and risky. There has to be some newness here, not necessarily the creation of a new system but some shift away from the old. It reminds me of the big fish in a small pond, small fish in a big pond metaphor. It is unlikely that you will ever reach the new pond without trying something different.

People often say that in order to achieve superior performance you need to be brave and have courage. The key word here is often, because it is not always the case. If we describe a need for something then it can limit the achievement of our goals. If you misspell goal you end up in an American gaol, and that isn't what we want. Perhaps we don't always need the courage to do something new, so to mention it could be inaccurate. Of course there will be times when being brave and courageous is required and when that time comes we can roll them out. Keep them on our radar but they do not need to be central to our thoughts.

Observation goes hand in hand with systems. Find a way to quantify and all qualify the performance changes you are making. First and foremost see them for yourself. Evidence and witnesses can be required to make the case for change. Be clear that it could come down to behaviors, and at a deeper level, beliefs. Keep an eye on your vitality, as this often significantly improves. How are your energy sources operating, soul, body, heart, mind and spirit. Energy levels racing, ideas, running, floating. 'Eufearia.' a mix of euphoria and fear. Euphoric, tinged with fear. Capturing all your great ideas. Delivering on what you believe. What feedback are you receiving? What feedback are you giving? How present have you become?

Seeing is believing. No, another chance to turn something on its head. Downside, upside down. Believing is seeing. A far more powerful statement. I experienced seeing is believing during my trip to Varanasi and the Ganges. Remember the locals in the Americas. They could see the boats of the conquistadors, they could not believe in them. So whilst observation might begin with seeing to truly observe one must then flip it and begin with believing. Truly believing in your goals as a coachee will enable you to see the progress you are making. Belief systems. Belief will generate an energy that has greater potency than the act of seeing. Another journey, from seeing is believing to believing is seeing. Your old paradigm might have holes in it. The artist has visited your house and spotted one of his abstract paintings on your wall. He carefully explains that you have hung it upside down. 180 degrees later and you have a new perception. Not the right one, simply a new one. Another one.

As the saying goes "when the pupil is ready the teacher will appear." When the pupil believes the teacher will appear. This is absolutely critical to coaching and why I believe developing coachability far outweighs the focus on the coach. If you believe, you are ready then your world class coach will turn up. They have probably been there all along, coming in and out of your life. Sometimes recognized, sometimes you had no clue they were there. Without belief you cannot see them. If the relationship is obvious enough for you to recognize them they might take the form of your worst enemy. They ask you a question, you cannot see where they are coming from. They suggest something, you lack belief.

One of our family friends is a politician and has been for many years. He is a man with tremendous presence and the profile I place with him due to his political status is one that he more than lives up to. When I was about 18 years old we were talking about my future career. His background was in careers advisory, so he was the ideal coach. Yet I was not the ideal coachee. I had yet to find my belief, or share his. Persistent questions and ideas frustrated me. Intent on getting a reaction he made me an offer, suggesting that I could spend some time in a school that he was attached to so that I could explore teaching options. I politely declined, without the belief I could not see.

Three years later I listened to him. I shared his absolute belief. I had many well meaning comments that day, attendees at Mum's funeral swirled around me like leaves in autumn. 'We lost a baby,' he explained. Matter of fact, yet terribly exposing for someone of such perceived power. Take a look at my life I am a lot like you. The tables had turned and he was now close enough to start a war. I was fixed by what he said. The leaves continued their swirl, nibbling at sandwiches, lightening the mood. A marker had been laid down, my belief started to grow. Death and birth in their own swirl, inseparable. He had always been there, now I could see that. Five years later when I moved up to London I was in his office with a job offer for the summer. I politely accepted, with belief I could see. I am no longer physically in his office, yet I feel as if I am. Holding his counsel, watching for defining moments and believing.

Take this belief and allow it to fill your space. This book is a space, like a room, empty, you need to fill it. By comparison the book takes up a tiny amount of space in the cosmos. Yet your belief can fill the cosmos, your world and the worlds of others. My words may or may not promote belief, yet it is certainly an invitation to do so. Fill it with your belief, not mine. Beyond this book is where the belief currently resides, tap into it like an irrigation project to nourish barren lands. Once you shine a light on it darkness will no longer prevail. Thus what is not in the book is more important than what is in the book. The book is merely part of the space, it is what you bring to it that counts.

At the time I was not sure how or why I had set out to complete seven marathons in seven days. I started and I finished. I hadn't even entered some strange marathon camp, it was a normal working week, a system of my own creation. When I wasn't working, I was running, when I wasn't running I was sleeping.

I had recently read *Survival of the Fittest* by *Mike Stroud* where he and *Sir Ranulph Fiennes* ran seven marathons in seven days on seven continents. I didn't have their travel budget but for some unknown reason I did have a similar goal. With another ultra marathon six weeks away I figured I would run three consecutive marathons, Friday to Sunday. Of course seven in seven entered my consciousness and I set out tentatively on a 294 kilometers/183 mile journey.

Marathon one was a 4.29 hour breeze. Summer had started so my only compliant was the heat and runners' tan that I was about to receive. At the start of marathon two my GPS broke so I had to complete the exact same route as the previous day, in fact this route would now need to be repeated for the other five London runs that were to follow. I adapted to my lack of timepiece by checking parking meters for GMT information. I came home in 4.49, I think. By Sunday the fatigue that would stay with me for the following four days set in. So in an effort to manage the week ahead I set out at a slower pace, 5.10 clocked off.

Monday was my tipping point, I knew if I could complete this one then seven should be in the bag. I was delivering a workshop in Cornwall, and it had rained all day. In the afternoon I battled with my first doubts. The weather, the hilly route and the headache that I was experiencing. I came back to some of the Buddhist mantras about suffering. What did I expect? It was enough to see me run my slowest marathon at 5.53 in persistent rain. I got back to my car at 11pm in the Cornish darkness, aching muscles and aching for bed. After a few hundred more miles of driving I was back in London for marathon number five. Craving greater cushioning I started out in new trainers, but they hadn't stretched enough and now I had a blackened big toe nail for my troubles. Attacking the route I wanted to make amends for the previous night's slow event and clocked 4.44. To my surprise my second fastest time of the seven, achieved on day five.

After delivering a coaching workshop on Wednesday, marathon six can only be remembered for the amount of *Vaseline* that was used. Where and what for shall be left untold, 5.05. Thursday would see me having to get up early to finish marathon seven and then drive to Cardiff for a meeting. Desperate to finish, desperate to walk, my mind or body took over and informed me that I had pulled my thigh muscle with five miles to go. I limped home in 5.50, it was hardly a heroe's welcome. Why my body held up so well for 178 miles but thought it necessary to reduce me to walking for the victory lap is still beyond explanation.

During the week itself I had recognized that my systems had to be second to none. Every piece of kit, energy gel and water bottle had its small yet vital function. Post marathon meals were all consumed in the bath to save time and promote a faster recovery. By the end of the week my kit had moved down two flights of stairs to be located next to the front door to save extra miles around the home. There was an awful lot of challenge, but bizarrely plenty of support. I knew that the seven days had called on mental strength, perhaps even more than physical capability. It wasn't until a month later that I started to understand why and how I had done it. I recognized that I completed this challenge because I both wanted and needed to be a part of a new system. Some of which is supporting, some of which is challenging. Want alone, or need alone would not have been enough to see me join the club. I slowly realized how much I wanted to achieve the magical number seven. I wanted to tell people about my trials and tribulations via texts and at the weekend. Somewhere around day four I recognised that I needed to complete my goal. I reasoned with myself that to achieve this challenge I would need a week off work and a support crew. I had a clear week and this just about translated into a need, a support. The time was now. Wants and needs combined, I had the recipe for success. The energy that they created was immensely powerful, until mile 178 at least. To put it another way my preferences and priorities were acting simultaneously, everything was synchronized. This was something that I was preferring to do and it was a priority to do it this week. All too often I see individuals sticking to their preferences. It is all very well to work with our gifts, but if we don't work with our priorities then welcome to the comfort zone.

If you are clear on your intent then you probably have your needs and priorities lined up, belief. Do not worry too much about your wants and preferences, your instinct will guide you so that you are supported and challenged. Do you want what you need? Do you need what you want?

It's not about seeing

When did you first identify your values?
When did you first take a stand for these values?
Who do you know?
Who else will benefit?
Which system are you progressing?
Who are these people?
Who is setting you up?
Who are you connecting?
How can you serve others?
What will I learn from you?
What will you learn from me?
How can you link two systems?
When will you be ready?

What do you believe in?
What can you see?
Do you want what you need?
Do you need what you want?

Chapter 9

Energy

A destination for now

I had just presented a workshop at one of the most prestigious conferences in the coaching calendar. Run by the same folk who provided the space for Martin and I to meet. Having spent enough time in the green room enjoying the food, freebies and networking I went for a wander in the exhibition area. On this rare occasion learning professionals can adopt a bricks and mortar existence with their exhibition stands, they quickly fall into the aggressive tactics that you will find on any high street. To avoid being caught by a well meaning gimmick I made a beeline for the cafe area. There was a swap shop zone, which I signed up for. I offered some free coaching in return for some research case studies. I spotted someone else's posting, 'free authentic leadership profiling...' I normally only get this excited in the same way when I see a new pair of running trainers enter the market. Authenticity and profiling, wow, this was a new one on me. A few minutes later I was speaking to Jaz who would become my coach for the next couple of years.

'So do you practice authenticity personally or do you work with others and their authentic self?' Jaz's tone suggestive as he was hoping for the later.

'I run authentic leadership and coaching programs,' his first question had caught me off guard. Surely he wanted me to engage in a swap so why the challenge. Off guard and challenged within minutes, not my default but in hindsight it is a beautiful thing. We met later that week for an hour, which led to a whole afternoon.

I was lured, carried away yet voluntarily proceeded to the

threshold of adventure. I had come close earlier in the year, but the recession put the stoppers on my *Neuro Linguistic Programming (NLP)* studies. I have always kept one eye on the future, spotting or sometimes even starting trends in my personal space. It did not take me long to recognize that Jaz's approach combined with his unique profiling tools could be the next *NLP*. The word guard comes back into the fold here. A sense that Jaz was a shadow presence guarding the way forward, he had created this product and was keen to protect it. He shared my psychometric profile and it appeared that I had earned the right to progress beyond the threshold. During that first afternoon I experienced an unfamiliar world, strangely intimate forces kept me transfixed. The tractor beam had been set, he was going to coach and supervise me to become one of his accredited coaches.

The following week I was sitting on his couch sometimes feeling threatened by tests, sometimes aided by his magical help. My profile reports would anchor questions around my life's purpose and vitality, being authentic and potential impact, my life's direction and resilience, spread of energy and the current phase of my life. Know your energy. Manage your energy. Develop your energy.

I was not put in a box, instead placed on a journey at a point in time and space. There was a mix of Eastern and Western philosophy in his global approach. Resistance was futile, again I was working with my priorities as well as my preferences. I would spend my first year with him being a coachee and the second year as coach, with Jaz as my supervisor.

As coachee I would always seek out extra dimensions with Jaz, still operating from the well held dimensions of space and time of course. As I have just mentioned priorities were one of these dimensions as I shifted my perceptions further from a world of preferences only. It would be the yin to the yang that Jaz would offer so often. Finesse and precision to my world view. Sure we all have preferences, my priorities however would soon lead to increased levels of energy.

We also worked with a narrative approach, "All of life comes to us in narrative form; it's a story we tell." *Zander* and *Zander*. This quote sums up narrative coaching perfectly. It privileges individual stories and personal experience, and as a coachee our job is to unpack these accounts. Taking a leaf out of *Michael White's* books, the originator of Narrative Therapy, we would externalize, re-author and remember conversations. Our conversations would form a story. Often like a good novel it might be complex and highly absorbing, allowing the space for readers to exercise their imagination to foster 'dramatic engagement.' This provided Jaz and myself to contribute to the story lines and appreciate the unfolding drama. We would fill in the gaps, connect events, discover motive and reconcile with the underlying theme of the story.

White uses maps as a reference point for his conversations. Describing a landscape of action (plot, time, sequence, circumstances, events) and a landscape of identity (realizations learnings knowledges, internal understandings). When we enter these landscapes we would attribute "a range of intentions and purposes to the actions of the protagonists and reaches conclusions about their character and identity."

When Jaz was peering into my landscape he would lead with the slightly risky question, 'what are you willing to die for?' He was encouraging me to develop my value proposition and in doing so to be more authentic. He would often present a view that I had not considered before. For example, like me he believed that we are often true and authentic to our current position. Then he would extend the view, 'are you being true and authentic to your potential position?' Another coaching question that I just love and fear in the same moment. One which fixes my gaze and calls for a different approach. Mindful of a future that has not happened, but encouraging a view that sits just beyond the present moment. Paradoxically one that we can ignore by being present, but one that we need to be present to. I love getting Jaz talking, ideas bounce off the walls like sunlight off glass, like philosophers we challenge, engaging creativity, spirituality almost. Never linear in our dialogue, always digression.

As allies in alchemy somewhere in our coaching I discovered a simple yet powerful tool in my armory, intention engineering. It's one of the best ways to harness energy. My plans, aims, designs, stretching purpose. Married with the action of working artfully to bring something about. We were skillful contrivers, originators and prime engineers of the approach.

That is the science, so let's explore the simplicity. Take an intention and engineer it. Carefully craft your language and state it, verbally written or both. A helpful starting point is to start with, 'I want to...' Dot, dot, dot fill in the gaps. For example, 'I want to boost innovation in my team.' 'I want to be a stronger player.' That's it. This simple statement is enough to harness your energy and develop results. Think like a pebble...

We drop our intent into the field of potentiality like a pebble into the sea. The ripples flow outward connecting with, and affecting, everything around it. The power of our intent in any given situation is a force to be recognized and harnessed authentically if we are to achieve what we hope to achieve in our lives. The way the power of intent operates is a natural law – it is one of the implications of quantum physics and will always function like this in any situation. It is how the world works.

These kind of intentions come from your core. When conversing with Jaz I was certainly developing my inner nature, the Japanese call this kind of personal development 'kokoro', literally meaning heart. I was mastering the technique but also perfecting the way of being that is consistent with coaching. Calm and grounded, learning being, not knowledge or technical skills. Spirit and standards. Holding the question, 'how do I be?' Embody and become part of the lineage. Like you, becoming the next generation of masters, be it coach or coachee. Our responsibility to pass on both the technical and mystical sides of the formula.

Western society has separated the process of developing a way of being from the process of learning. In most management or sporting texts there is little or no importance placed on how you have to be in order to improve performance. The emphasis, unfortunately is on skills and technique. Valuable as a starting point but depreciating towards the end goal. Set out by making a commitment. To become a great coachee, the first question to ask, therefore, is not 'what do I do?' but 'how do I be?'

I am signing up for ultra marathons over 50 miles in length, flying through my work and achieving everything that I want in my personal life. Maybe I know why energy feels like my destination, it's because of these results. It's where everything comes together, my possibilities, perception and performance. Being authentic, open to change, harnessing emotions, curious, challenged, questioning, goal orientated, systems led and energetic. I promise you I don't do this on purpose I rely on synchronicities or coincidences. The one word I use to describe this place is being - who are you being? Like any good question as soon as you get near to composing a response you need to readjust your standards.

Energetic performance

Knowing, managing and developing our energy are not permanent accomplishments, rather a walk among flowers. Remember it's the 'journey not the destination.' There is no possession, only the lifelong search to maintain yourself within the boundaries of a system of beliefs. There is so much to explore here that it might feel like a destination at times. I am sure you will still be traveling but for now it's in one country.

A well referenced area framed by quantum physics and the laws of nature. Far more reassuring than some practices that lack some of these boundaries and is governed by man made laws.

Energy is all we have so it makes total sense to develop it. Why bother developing your project management skills (goals) if you have not got the energy to match?

The bodies drawn up by *McTaggart, Chopra, Bohm, Zukav* and *Byrne* are all great reference points. The one to really bridge the gap between knowledge and practice was *Simmons* who I talked briefly about earlier. Her approach can be likened to the base camps that are required to climb a mountain. You need to tackle the climb step by step, moving up to one of these camps and grounding yourself by coming down for periods of acclimatization. Up and down, and so on until you have the energy for summit day. Developing personal energy is as important as tying onto ropes properly and predicting weather windows.

Base camp I - everything is energy. We are all energy vibrating at different frequencies, this book, what you are sitting, standing or lying on, what you can see over your shoulder. The commas and etc here are endless. Enter base camp I and be warmed and amazed by this significance. Appreciate the interconnected nature of life and the potentiality of our intentions.

Base camp II - we can influence our personal energy. Pitch your tent around the five energy sources - soul, body, heart, mind and spirit. Be conscious of the physical tasks that can shift our energy but also non physical, such as designing intentions for yourself and others.

Camp III - we can influence the energy of others. By being in a calm state we can calm others. Obviously by what we say but more powerfully by our energy. Remember camp I, we are all energy. Therefore, our energy travels between these different systems just like electricity arrives at your home. Animals are incredibly susceptible to our energy, for example fear. They have less to go on, they cannot read our facial expressions or words like we can, yet they can read us perfectly by focusing on our energy alone. We too can read each other's energy. Only we are a victim of our success, as other observations that we can make that animals can't get in the way.

Camp IV - you can also influence the energy of inanimate objects. At the high camp you are preparing for the final days summit push. Sleep might be uneasy, your appetite plummets and even the simplest tasks like making a cup of tea or going to the toilet turn into a mission. Remember you might have to return to base camp before pitching your tent here with ease. Yes, that laptop, car or DIY project can all be influenced by our energy. Breathing is your preventative measure here, stay calm, relaxed and like water seek a smooth passage. Take a deep breath, relax and open up your energy sources.

An easy way to make your way up and down these camps is to work with the present moment. My favorite piece of information in my profiling reports with Jaz was a line that should resemble the traditional bell curve. Low to the left and right, most of the distribution in the middle. On the left you would find the past, in the middle the present and to the right the future. This begs the question; where is your energy? Locked up and missing in the past which identifies a challenge, our active energy in the present or reserved or idle in the future identifying an opportunity. Past, present and future.

If I was recommending any shift in energy this would be a great place to start. Yes, focus some attention on reviewing the past and looking ahead to what's around the corner but keep firmly routed on the present. Right here, right now. *Tolle* asks the questions that allows this precision. 'what have you achieved in the past?' If you were to answer this question then no doubt you would be drawing up a long list. A long list that sadly is imprecise. None of what you have on that glorious award winning list is accurate. Why? Because you did not achieve that in the past. You achieved it in the present. The same flippant answer applies to the question 'what will you achieve in the future?' Wonderfully grounding. *Tolle's* next question is 'right now, what is the problem?' More inaccurate responses;

'yesterday I had a really bad team meeting, sales weren't great for our last quarter and I think there might be a department restructure round the corner.' Hold the question and accurately compose your answer and watch your past and future problems slip away allowing you to open the taps for your present energy flow.

One of the best exponents of living in the present was the cyclist and seven times winner of the *Tour De France, Lance Armstrong*. Many people thought that his cancer treatment had provided his body with similar effects to drug enhancements. They were right, *Armstrong* was on drugs, he took them every day. Having experienced near death he trained and raced in the now. Treating each wet, cold and mountainous training day like it was his last. Sure he made technical improvements like losing weight and improving his climbing skills by cranking up his cadence. It was the mind and body changes that were to be his fuel. In his own words he 'maximizes time.'

One infamous training session in France describes how towards the top of a climb his team finds out that the summit is covered in snow. There would be no way to descend the pass on the other side. As the message reaches *Armstrong*, in the drizzle he replies, 'then we will go back down and repeat this climb.' His team had sensed an early finish but the ever present champion had denied them, just as he would his challengers.

Goals can be our gaol here. 'My coach thinks I haven't worked on my fitness enough or matured as a player so I need to work on that.' Or, 'I think I need to collaborate more to achieve next year's sales targets.' All well meaning glimpses forward and backwards, but potentially misleading goals for coachees. At the time of writing so many strategies have been kyboshed in a matter of weeks and months due to the global recession, how can we possibly prepare a business plan that will serve us for such a long period of time. I heard a story about one organization that reviews their strategy every Monday morning. Good on them, they are living in the now.

So if energy exists in the present, what form does it take? Like the *Karate Kid* you are prepared for this one. Energy flows through your soul, body, heart, mind and spirit. Locate your reserves of energy and any arid areas. You might need to set up better irrigation systems. A reservoir of intellectual energy for example might be called on to nourish a famine in your physical domain. Focus on the adjoining energy sources if you want to make a shift. Do not just focus on the domain that needs attention, also focus on the sources that sit underneath it. Grounded energy (soul) forms the bottom or foundation with creative energy (spirit) sitting at the top. Again a more Eastern than Western view.

In the West if I injure my knee I would apply the RICE principle, rest, ice, compression and elevation. Again all well meaning attempts to alleviate the situation. I could also be looking at my energy that sits underneath my knee. Stretch the calf and pay attention to footwear and gait. I suppose we are back to multiple systems again. A coachee must be willing and patient to search in areas beyond the obvious.

There is one risk to energy potential and that comes from the ego. Not just something that *Freud* came up with, it exists. This is part of the body, perhaps located in the brain that feeds on pain, discomfort and suffering. It is the little devil on our shoulder that can leave so many people stuck in victim mode. 'how are you today?' 'not bad' comes the reply. Well, that reply comes right from your ego and can jeopardize your energetic state. An overriding ego sits with the people who are always busy, stressed (in the non medical form) and constantly in and out of drama. They lead their life like a soap opera moving from one big deal to another, their ego feeds on this because they allow it to. A client recently exclaimed, 'things used to be manic but now they are insane.' Too much attachment, more language games. Simply identify the ego next time it surfaces and your reservoirs of energy will remain pure and rich. Allow it to enter for too long and you energy supplies will become polluted and stagnant.

The ego sits within another concept we have looked at, from and formless. Around 4,000 BC our earliest ancestors were commonly known as hunters and gatherers. A foraging society where most or all food is obtained from wild plants and animals. During this period the ego was formless, we were engaged in music, storytelling, art and sex. Then society changed and began to take form. Agriculture displaced foraging, materialistic rise. Being at one with nature, owning nature. The next trigger was environmental factors, desertification as temperatures increased and rainfall decreased. Again shifting our way of life, this time to a nomadic one. Migration from the once fertile African continent to agricultural hotspots. Communities protect, others conquer. War, patriarchy and inequality now define our form.

Challenges will continue, as will support. You can sustain this, like running, it is a case for how long? Too short and you will miss development opportunities, too long and you have had too much of a good thing. Like my long shore drift example, it is time for a gravity assisted break. Ground yourself, whilst being conscious of the next development activity.

As you wander, the hole is always there but it does not call you. Sometimes the environment is quiet, sometimes you will receive a few messages. There might be drama, but do not perceive it in that way. The seas are calm because you navigate this new land in the present moment, keeping a lid on your ego. You have developed coachability. If you get too far ahead of yourself or continue to look behind you then you might find yourself washed up on the rocks. You have made a different choice. If you let your ego surface, it will in turn create a different surface. Changing the landscape, illusory in nature. 'I don't mind what happens.' This hardly feels like a call to arms or rallying term to defeat the cause. More motto then battle cry. Mantra, humble and incredibly powerful.

You have moved far beyond understanding, for understanding

is the booby prize. The writings of *Carlos Castaneda* come back to me, "To move between these two points you call understanding. You've been doing that all your life. If you say you understand my knowledge, you have done nothing new." There is nothing to understand, understanding is only a very small affair. Choose your own co-ordinates...

Understanding, doing, being.

Consider, challenge, change.

Possibilities, perception, performance.

Aware, adapt, action.

Transact, transform, transcend.

Observation, programming, let it happen, observation.

History, winning strategy, predictable future, possible future.

Be of knowledge, have an ally, your ally has a rule and the rule was corroborated by special consensus.

Wait, harness, expand, broaden, partner, target, broadcast, relate, connect, control.

It's not about the past or future

How do I be?

What is your ambition?

Where is your focus?

What does the journey look like?

Is there a destination?

What is energy?

How will you influence your energy?

How can you influence the energy of others?

When do you allow you ego to surface?

How can you re-charge?

What do you need to attend to physically?

How are you feeling?

How can you nourish your mind?

Where can you be creative?

Right now, what is the problem?
"I'm moving
I'm coming
Can you hear, what I hear
It's calling you my dear
Out of reach
(Take me to my beach)
I can hear it, calling you
I'm coming not drowning
Swimming closer to you
(Take me to my beach)"
Pure Shores - All Saints

PART 6 – MASTER OF TWO WORLDS

There isn't anywhere else to visit now. The road has split, should I choose right or left. No, this is the wrong question. I should choose both right and left. Energy feels like the destination, maybe it is just a fork in a road that we will linger at for some time. Passing back and forth across the divisions, nothing too mystical just coach and coachee.

A glance backwards but we are still operating in the now. Coaches who enter the coaching relationship raring to go. Trained, qualified, accredited, supervised, well read with skills and models bursting from up their sleeves. Great, this is great and must always be the case for coaching to flourish. A pro that creates a con, a gap. Bridging these gaps will take time. Just some time for the coachee, not in equal weighting to the coach but something to even it up. An investment that can accelerate the learning and bring quicker and deeper results. Appreciating the skills required to be an effective coachee, making better more informed choices. Informing coachees, not an excuse to abdicate. Meet the needs of the present without compromising the ability of the coachee to meet their own needs in the future. A success.

Meet the needs of the present and develop the ability of the coachee to meet their own needs in the future. An overwhelming success. A journey best tackled when both coach and coachee attend to their development prior to setting out. Neither top down nor bottom up. Simultaneous. Otherwise the energy will only reach so far. Messages get diluted or stuck.

Accelerating the relationship, delivering greater impact and improving our return on investment. Pre work for coachees to develop readiness for coaching. An opportunity to develop the skills that are required of effective coachees. Bring it on. Whatever will come up will come up, be bold, take a stand and bring it on.

Return to our map when we need to, otherwise we run the risk of proceeding haphazardly with little or no reference points. This gives us the opportunity to review our past successes, locate our present location and map out our future intentions. Possibilities, perception and performance once formed our timeline. Now you can consider these co-ordinates at any time.

Consider *Possibilities* Aware Possibilities - ideas, potential, wonder, be curious and promise. Considering all your different possibilities, awareness of yourself and others will increase. Considering - thinking about, bearing in mind, believing, deeming, judging and regarding. As an indictor of your success you will be more aware, conscious, sensitive, alert, attentive, awake, sentient and responsive. Valuing authenticity, change and emotions.

Challenging *Perception* Adapt Perception - insight, reading, acuity, discernment, observation and sensitivity.Challenging your perception, adapting yourself accordingly. A considering nature that has now turned into a challenging one. Willing to confront, daring, disputing, testing, defying, facing, facing up and being brave. You have already harnessed one of nature's most powerful energies, adaptation. Become accustomed, change, familiarize yourself, get a feel for, get used to, acclimatize, find your feet, settle in and adjust. Valuing curiosity, challenge and questions.

Changing *Performance* Action Performance - present, display, accomplish, task, action, operation, capabilities, capacity. Changing your performance, taking action. A change in your behavior. Altering, alternating, breaking, exchanging, modifying, varying, transforming, revolutionizing, adjusting and amending. The bottom line identified by action. Act, deed, achievement, accomplish and feat. Valuing goals, systems and energy. "Karma police, arrest this man He talks in myths He buzzes like a fridge He's like a detuned radio" You have entered a new world. Two worlds. Coach and coachee. A master of both worlds, defined by

Nietzsche as a cosmic dancer, not resting in a single spot, but gaily, lightly, turning and leaping from one position to another. Now that you have mastered being a coachee you can really master being a coach. You can travel safely from now on...

Journeys that began in the wrong place. The ray of light, intense orange and red colors that are the coach. The earth has rotated many a time since and after a while you notice a different display. The separation of orange colors in the direction from the sun and the blue components scattered from the surrounding sky. The trailing edge of the coach has slowly disappeared below the horizon in the West.

Now there are two suns in the sunset, coach and coachee. You can see them both, and be them both. Like a planet in its elliptical orbit around the Sun, we are paired revolutions around each other. We are paired revelations around each other. A solstice to be enjoyed in summer or winter, reaching our extremes and never standing still. Our ideas are refracted, still visible below the horizon. Appearing larger in the distance, an optical illusion.

As a ray of white sunlight travels through the atmosphere, some of the colors are scattered out of the beam by air molecules and airborne particles. This changes our final color, shorter wavelength components, such as blue and green, scatter more strongly. Preferentially removed from the beam. The path is longer, only the longer wavelength orange and red hues remain. Reddened. The halo of white light is around you no longer. It is around me. It is around us both. Saddened. Yet our colors are more brilliant than ever, more particles exist. Our afterglow burns strongly. We are reaching higher altitudes, reflecting and striking, long after sunset. A green flash rarely seen.

PART 7 - AFTERWORD

'How many items of luggage are you checking in?' she asks. 'One.' I reply, placing it on the belt. 'Have you got any of these items in your hand luggage?' she remains locked in on her screen, but I know where to look. 'Nope.' I shake my head and glance sideways, trying to hurry up the process.'Did you pack your bag yourself?''Yes.' I delay. 'And, no one could have interfered with it,' I smile, chuckle knowingly.

My bag is packed I am ready to go, I have everything I need. Not just for this trip to Spain but for being a coachee and now for being a coach. I did pack my bag myself and for that I should take credit. Could anyone have interfered with it. Oh yes. Let me see, Mr. Sanders could have, as could Rob and Emma. Lee and Mo got involved, leaving it wide open for Jaz to be the overwhelming interference that he is. In many ways my ties to the bag packers are severed as I set off on another journey. In many ways the umbilical cord could not be tighter. I have discovered a benign power everywhere, supporting me in my passage. The power is within me. I feel part of this world but I don't feel part of it. I need to develop both feelings. I cannot loose touch, I have experienced that before. Too much time in the red zone and I might not make it out.

More questions as I remove most of what I am wearing at security. Another chuckle as I am reminded that I will soon be on the aforementioned beach.

I didn't come here to tell you how this is going to end, I came here to tell you how this is going to begin. More afterworld than afterword, without rules and controls lacking borders or boundaries. A world where anything is possible. Where we go from there is a choice I leave to you.

There will be more, but I don't know what that is right now. Deep down I know that if I can crack the individual context then

I could tackle coaching culture. I have a nagging sense that it's not about the team. A sneaky suspicion that it's not about the leader. Starting not ending. Series, trilogy. The desert has now turned to sea.

I don't know where I will be but come and find me. Once removed, then we will become complete. Search engine, website presence, social media hang out. It's not about the coach, an online experience that is quickly taking shape. Alliances being built that will create a workshop space. I invite you all to come to the edge. Dot, dot, dot...

"Come to the edge, he said
We are afraid, they said
Come to the edge, he said
They came to the edge
He pushed them and they flew"
Guilliame Apollinaire

References

Bach, R & Munson, R (1973) Jonathan Livingston Seagull: A story, London: Pan Books Ltd.

Beanies, J (1997) Biomimicry: Innovation Inspired by Nature, Great Britain: William Morrow.

Bohm, D (2002) Wholeness and the Implicate Order, UK: Routledge Classics.

Byrne, R (2006) The Secret, London: Simon & Schuster Ltd.

Campbell, J (1993) The Hero with a Thousand Faces, London: Fontana Press.

Carroll, L & Tensile J (1992) Alice in Wonderland, UK: Wordsworth Editions Ltd.

Castaneda, C (2004) The Teachings of Don Juan: A Yaqui Way of Knowledge, London: Penguin.

Chopra, D (2000) The Way Of The Wizard: 20 Lessons for Living a Magical Life, London: Rider.

Coach Carter (2005) DVD.

Cohen, M (2012) Tao - The Way of the Coach, Kindle Edition

Dryer, D & Dryer K (2008) Chirunning: A Revolutionary Approach to Effortless, Injury-Free Running, London: Pocket Books.

Freire, P & Ramos, MB (1996) Pedagogy of the Oppressed, London: Penguin.

Gallagher, BJ & Ventura, S (2004) Who are They Anyway? A Tale of Achieving Success at Work Through Personal Accountability, London: Kaplan Trade.

Karate Kid (2007) DVD.Goleman, D (2005) Emotional Intelligence, London: Bantam Books.Klein, N (1998) Time to Think: Listening to Ignite the Human Mind, London: Cassell Illustrated.

Man on Wire (2008) DVD.McGonigal, J (2011) Reality is Broken. Why Games Make Us Better and How They Can Change the

World, London: Jonathan Cape.

McTaggart, L (2003) The Field: The Quest for the Secret Force of the Universe, London: Element.

Naipaul, VS (1991) India: A Million Mutinies Now, London: Penguin.

Pirsig, RM (1974) Zen and the Art of Motorcycle Maintenance, London: Vintage.

Simmons, A (2009) Quantum Skills for Coaches, A Handbook for Working with Energy and the Body-mind in Coaching, UK: Word4Word.

Sogyal Rinpoche (1996) The Tibetan Book of Living and Dying, India: Rupa.

Star Wars Episode V: The Empire Strikes Back (2006) DVD.

Stroud, M (2004) Survival Of The Fittest: The Anatomy of Peak Physical Performance, London: Yellow Jersey.

Tolle, E (2001) The Power of Now: A Guide to Spiritual Enlightenment, UK: Hodder Paperbacks.

The Matrix (1999) DVD.

Wheatley, M (2001) Leadership and the New Science: Discovering Order in Chaotic World, CA: Berrett-Koehler.

White, M (2007) Maps of Narrative Practice, NY: WW Norton & Company Inc.

Whitmore, J (2003) Coaching for Performance. GROWing People, Performance and Purpose, Third Edition, London: Nicholas Brealey Publishing Limited.

Zander, R and Zander B (2000) The Art of Possibility: Transforming Professional and Personal Life, London: Penguin.

Zukav, G (1991) The Dancing Wu Li Masters: An Overview of the New Physics, London: Rider.

About the author

It's Not About the Coach is Stuart's first book. As a coach, facilitator and consultant he has an innate ability to open up new spaces in coaching, teams and leadership. He values culture, authenticity and energy in all aspects of his life. He lives in London with his wife and daughter.

www.stormbeach.co.uk

stuart@stormbeach.co.uk

www.facebook.com/storm.beach

www.twitter.com/StormBeach

www.tumblr.com/blog/itsnotaboutthecoach

**BUSINESS
BOOKS**

Business Books encapsulates the freshest thinkers and the most
successful practitioners in the areas of marketing, management,
economics, finance and accounting, sustainable and ethical
business, heart business, people management, leadership,
motivation, biographies, business recovery and development
and personal/executive development.